CATHOLIC PETER

St. Joseph Sunday and Daily Missal :
Prayerbook and Hymns for 2024

First edition

This book was professionally typeset on Reedsy.
Find out more at reedsy.com

Contents

IV Liturgical Calendar

V Devotion and prayers

VI Liturgical Hymns

VII Additional Resources

I

Introduction

Welcome, dear reader, to the sacred sanctuary of the St. Joseph Sunday and Daily Missal Hymnal and Prayerbook 2024. Within the hallowed pages of this revered tome, you will discover a divine invitation to embark on a journey of faith, prayer, and spiritual enlightenment. As you turn each page, may your heart be lifted, your soul be nourished, and your spirit be rejuvenated by the timeless wisdom and grace encapsulated within its covers

1

Welcome to the St. Joseph Sunday and Daily Missal Hymnal and Prayerbook 2024

In the hustle and bustle of our modern lives, amidst the cacophony of worldly distractions, it is all too easy to lose sight of the profound significance of daily prayer and devotion. Yet, it is precisely in these moments of quiet contemplation, in the whisper of a heartfelt prayer, that we find solace, strength, and communion with the divine.

The St. Joseph Sunday and Daily Missal Hymnal and Prayerbook 2024 stands as a steadfast companion on your spiritual journey, a beacon of light amidst the darkness, guiding you ever closer to the loving embrace of our Heavenly Father. With its meticu- lously curated selection of prayers, hymns, and reflections, it offers a sanctuary of solace in a world fraught with uncertainty and turmoil.

Within its sacred pages, you will find the rich tapestry of

Catholic tradition woven seamlessly with the rhythms of the liturgical year. From the solemnity of Advent to the jubilation of Easter, each season invites us to immerse ourselves fully in the mystery of Christ's redemptive love, to walk in His footsteps, and to proclaim His Gospel to all the ends of the earth.

But the St. Joseph Sunday and Daily Missal Hymnal and Prayerbook 2024 is more than just a compendium of prayers and hymns. It is a testament to the enduring power of faith, a testament to the enduring presence of God in our lives, even in the midst of our darkest trials and tribulations.

As you delve into its sacred pages, may you find comfort in the embrace of the saints who have gone before us, may you find inspiration in the words of holy men and women who have borne witness to the transformative power of God's grace. And may you, dear reader, be drawn ever deeper into the heart of Christ, who is the Way, the Truth, and the Life.

So, with hearts uplifted and spirits renewed, let us embark together on this sacred pilgrimage through the pages of the St. Joseph Sunday and Daily Missal Hymnal and Prayerbook 2024. May its words be a balm to our weary souls, a beacon of hope in our darkest hours, and a source of boundless grace and consolation for all who Find solace within the tender embrace of our Divine Father.

Welcome, esteemed reader, to the journey of a lifetime.. Welcome to the St. Joseph Sunday and Daily Missal Hymnal and Prayerbook 2024.

2

The Importance of Daily Prayer

In the serene embrace of our faith, we embark on a sacred journey within the pages of the St. Joseph Sunday and Daily Missal Hymnal and Prayerbook 2024. Within these hallowed passages lies the heartbeat of Catholic devotion, where each prayer, hymn, and reflection breathes life into our souls, nurturing our spirits with divine grace and boundless love.

In the tapestry of our lives, daily prayer is the thread that weaves our connection to the divine. It is the gentle whisper that guides us through the labyrinth of existence, offering solace in times of despair and illumination in moments of darkness. Through the rhythm of prayer, we find sanctuary midst the chaos, a sacred sanctuary where our hearts commune with the Almighty.

Within the folds of daily prayer lies a sacred communion with the divine, a sacred communion that transcends the boundaries of time and space. It is a divine dialogue, where our souls dance in harmony with the Creator, offering gratitude for the blessings bestowed upon us and seeking solace in moments of tribulation.

In the quietude of prayer, we find refuge from the cacophony of the world, a tranquil haven where our spirits soar on the wings of faith.

Each prayer uttered is a sacred invocation, a beckoning to the divine to dwell within our midst. It is a testament to our faith, a testament that resonates through the corridors of eternity, echoing the timeless devotion of saints and sinners alike. Through the sacrament of prayer, we partake in a divine communion, where our souls are nourished by the bread of heaven and the cup of salvation.

In the sanctuary of prayer, we are enveloped by the divine presence, a presence that transcends the limitations of human understanding. It is a sacred communion, where our hearts are laid bare before the throne of grace, seeking solace in the embrace of the Almighty. Through the gentle whispers of prayer, we find solace in moments of despair, strength in times of weakness, and hope in the face of adversity.

Daily prayer is the cornerstone of our faith, a sacred ritual that binds us to the eternal mysteries of the divine. It is a testament to our devotion, a testament that reverberates through the annals of history, echoing the timeless supplications of prophets and patriarchs. Through the sacred rhythms of prayer, we are transported beyond the confines of mortal existence, ascending to the celestial realms where angels dance and saints sing praises to the Most High.

In the sanctuary of prayer, we discover the true essence of our humanity, a humanity that is imbued with divine grace and boundless love. It is a sacred journey, where our souls are transformed by the gentle touch of the Holy Spirit, igniting the flames of faith that burn brightly within our hearts. Through the sacrament of prayer, we are united with the divine, bound together by the cords of love that stretch across the vast expanse of eternity.

As we embark on this sacred journey within the pages of the St. Joseph Sunday and Daily Missal Hymnal and Prayerbook 2024, let us embrace the transformative power of daily prayer. Let us surrender our hearts to the divine, allowing the gentle whispers of the Holy Spirit to guide us on this sacred pilgrimage of faith. And let us bear witness to the wondrous mysteries of the divine, as we journey together towards the eternal light that beckons us home.

In the sanctuary of prayer, we find solace in the embrace of the divine, strength in the presence of the Almighty, and hope in the promise of eternal salvation. Let us, therefore, heed the call of our hearts and embark on this sacred journey with faith, hope, and love as our guiding stars. For in the sanctuary of prayer, we discover the true essence of our humanity, a humanity that is forever intertwined with the divine.

So let us lift our voices in prayer, let us raise our hearts in praise, and let us journey together towards the eternal light that shines within us all. For in the sanctuary of prayer, we are united with the divine, bound together by the cords of love that stretch across the vast expanse of eternity.

3

Understanding the Liturgical Year

In the rhythmic cadence of the Catholic faith, the liturgical year stands as a sacred journey, a tapestry woven with threads of tradition, celebration, and spiritual growth. As we embark on this divine odyssey, it is imperative to grasp the profound significance embedded within the seasons, feasts, and solemnities that adorn our calendar.

1. Advent: A Season of Hope and Preparation

The liturgical year unfurls its initial chapter with the hushed anticipation of Advent. Like the tender whisper of a distant star, Advent beckons believers to await the coming of the Messiah with hearts wide open and spirits ablaze with hope. Spanning the four weeks preceding Christmas, Advent invites the faithful into a sacred space of preparation, reflection, and joyful expectancy. Midst the hustle and bustle of secular festiv- ities, the Church calls her children to pause, to ponder, and to prepare the manger of their souls for the coming of Emmanuel, God-with-us. Through the lighting of Advent candles, the chanting of ancient hymns, and the solemn proclamation of prophetic scriptures, the faithful journey through the twilight of anticipation, eagerly awaiting the dawn of Christ's nativity.

2. Christmas: Celebrating the Birth of Our Savior

With the midnight hour of Christmas Eve, the liturgical year crescendos into a symphony of jubilation and wonder. In the tender innocence of a newborn babe lying in a humble manger, the fullness of God's love is made manifest to humanity. Christmas, the feast of the Incarnation, beckons believers to gaze upon the face of the Infant Christ with awe and reverence, to behold the mystery of God made flesh. Through the singing of carols, the adoration of the Christ Child, and the sharing of festive meals, the Church rejoices in the dawning of salvation history. In the embrace of family and the warmth of community, the true meaning of Christmas shines forth: a divine invitation to encounter the infinite love of the Father, poured out upon the world in the person of His Son.

3. Lent: A Time of Reflection and Repentance

As the chill of winter gives way to the gentle stirrings of spring, the Church enters into the solemn season of Lent. With ashes upon our foreheads and contrition in our hearts, believers embark on a forty-day pilgrimage of fasting, prayer, and almsgiving. Lent, a sacred season of penance and purification, calls the faithful to journey into the desert of their souls, to confront the shadows of sin and to embrace the light of grace. Through the disciplines of prayer, fasting, and almsgiving, believers unite their sufferings with the redemptive sacrifice of Christ, journeying with Him along the via dolorosa to the foot of the Cross. In the solemnity of Holy Week, the Church enters into the mystery of Christ's passion, death, and resurrection, culminating in the triumphant celebration of Easter.

4. Easter: Rejoicing in the Resurrection

With the rising of the sun on Easter Sunday, the Church bursts forth in exultant joy, proclaiming the victory of life over death, of love over sin. Easter, the feast of feasts, stands as the pinnacle of the liturgical year, the radiant dawn of redemption breaking forth upon a world ensnared by darkness. Through the solemn rites of the Easter Vigil and the jubilant strains of the Gloria, believers are invited to share in the paschal mystery, to die with Christ and rise with Him to newness of life. In the sacraments of initiation, the waters of baptism, and the bread of eternal life, the Church celebrates the triumph of grace, welcoming new members into the communion of saints. With hearts ablaze with the fire of the Holy Spirit, believers go forth as heralds of the Good News, bearing witness to the resurrection hope that
transforms lives and renews the face of the earth.

5. Ordinary Time: Embracing the Mission of Christ

As the Easter season gives way to the gentle rhythm of Ordinary Time, the Church enters into a season of growth, of maturation, of mission. Ordinary Time, far from being mundane or routine, is imbued with the radiant splendor of Christ's presence, unfolding His saving mysteries in the midst of everyday life. Through the liturgical readings and feasts of Ordinary Time, believers are invited to journey with Christ through the unfolding tapestry of salvation history, to walk in His footsteps and to embrace His mission of love and mercy. In the ordinary moments of daily life – in the laughter of children, the kindness of strangers, the forgiveness of enemies – the extraordinary grace of God is made manifest, transforming hearts and renewing the face of the earth.

In conclusion, the liturgical year stands as a sacred journey of faith, an invitation to encounter the living God in the midst of human history.

Through the seasons of Advent, Christmas, Lent, Easter, and Ordinary Time, believers are drawn ever deeper into the mystery of Christ's saving love, journeying with Him along the pathways of grace to the eternal banquet of heaven. May we embrace this sacred journey with hearts ablaze with faith, minds illumined by truth, and spirits enkindled by love, that we may truly become living witnesses to the Gospel of Jesus Christ in the world today.

II

Sunday Missal

*In the ethereal embrace of a Sunday morning, as
sunlight dances through stained-glass windows, we
are called to embark on a sacred journey. The Sunday
Missal, a revered companion, unveils the tapestry of
divine mysteries woven within the heart of the liturgy.
With each turn of its hallowed pages, we traverse the
landscape of faith, guided by ancient rituals and
timeless truths.*

4

The Liturgy of the Word

In the sacred journey of the Sunday liturgy, the Liturgy of the Word emerges as a profound moment of divine encounter, a symphony of Scripture where the voice of God resonates with the hearts of the faithful. As we gather in the embrace of our faith communities, the Liturgy of the Word beckons us to listen, to ponder, and to respond to the living Word proclaimed midst us.

At the heart of the Liturgy of the Word lies the proclamation of sacred Scripture, a tapestry woven with threads of divine revelation and human experience. The liturgical cycle unveils a mosaic of readings, meticulously selected to guide the faithful through the narrative of salvation history. From the majestic psalms echoing the soul's deepest yearnings to the prophetic voices that challenge and inspire, each passage holds a sacred invitation to encounter the living God.

The first reading, often drawn from the Old Testament, serves as a bridge connecting the faith of ancient Israel with the life and teachings of Jesus Christ. Through the lens of tradition and prophecy, we trace the footsteps of our spiritual ancestors, finding echoes of their struggles, triumphs, and enduring faith in our own pilgrimage of discipleship.

Following the ancient tradition of the Church, the Responsorial Psalm emerges as a liturgical response to the Word proclaimed. Set to melodies that stir the soul and lyrics that echo the psalmist's cry, the Responsorial Psalm becomes a communal prayer, uniting the voices of the faithful in praise, lament, and supplication.

As the liturgy unfolds, the second reading invites us into the apostolic witness, offering insights into the early Christian communities and the enduring relevance of their teachings for our lives today. From the epistles of St. Paul to the pastoral wisdom of the Catholic epistles, each reading invites us to discern the timeless truths that shape our identity as followers of Christ..

Finally, the Gospel acclamation heralds the arrival of the Gospel, the very heart of the Liturgy of the Word. With hearts attentive and spirits receptive, we rise to greet the Word made flesh, whose teachings illuminate our path and whose presence ignites the fire of faith within us.

In the solemn proclamation of the Gospel, the assembly stands as a living testament to the enduring power of God's Word. With reverence and awe, we listen as the deacon or priest unveils the sacred text, inviting us to enter into dialogue with the living Word who speaks to us through the pages of Scripture.

As the Gospel narrative unfolds, we are transported to the dusty roads of Galilee, the bustling streets of Jerusalem, and the tranquil shores of the Sea of Galilee. Through vivid imagery and poignant parables, Jesus beckons us to journey with Him, to wrestle with His teachings, and to embrace the radical demands of discipleship.

But the Liturgy of the Word is not merely a passive encounter with ancient texts; it is a transformative encounter with the living God who speaks to us in the here and now. As we listen with open hearts and minds, the Word takes root within us, challenging our assumptions, comforting our sorrows, and inspiring us to live lives of holiness and compassion.

And so, as the final words of the Gospel fade into silence, we are invited to respond—to respond with hearts aflame, minds renewed, and spirits emboldened by the transformative power of God's Word. Through hymns of praise, prayers of intercession, and acts of contrition, we offer ourselves anew to the One who calls us by name, inviting us to become living witnesses to the Word made flesh.

In the Liturgy of the Word, we encounter the living God who speaks to us in the stillness of our hearts, inviting us to embark on a journey of faith, hope, and love. As we heed the divine summons, may we be transformed by the Word proclaimed, becoming living reflections of Christ's love in the world.

This is the essence of the Liturgy of the Word—a sacred encounter, a divine dialogue, a transformative journey that unfolds week by week, drawing us ever closer to the heart of God.

May we approach this holy encounter with reverence and awe, eager to receive the Word who speaks to us with love beyond measure.

5

The Liturgy of the Eucharist

In the heart of Catholic worship lies the sacred ritual of the Liturgy of the Eucharist. This profound and solemn moment within the Mass encapsulates the essence of our faith, transcending time and space to unite believers with the divine presence of Christ himself. As we delve into the depths of this sacred rite, we are called to journey through the layers of symbolism, tradition, and spiritual significance that infuse every aspect of the Eucharistic celebration.

At the outset of the Liturgy of the Eucharist, the faithful are invited to offer their hearts and minds in preparation for the miraculous transformation that is about to unfold before them. The priest, vested in the sacred garments of his office, stands as a humble conduit, bridging the earthly realm with the heavenly banquet. With reverence and awe, the congregation gathers around the altar, their hearts uplifted in anticipation of the sacred mystery about to be revealed.

The Offertory, a poignant moment of solemnity and reverence, marks the beginning of the Liturgy of the Eucharist. As the faithful present their gifts of bread and wine, ordinary elements of sustenance are transformed into vessels of divine grace through the invocation of the Holy Spirit. The simple offerings of the faithful symbolize the entirety of creation, infused with the divine presence of God's love and providence.

As the priest elevates the sacred host and chalice, the congregation is invited to join in silent adoration, recognizing the profound mystery of Christ's presence among them. In this moment of sublime transcendence, time seems to stand still as heaven and earth converge in a symphony of divine love and redemption. The faithful are reminded of Christ's sacrificial offering on the cross, his body broken and blood shed for the salvation of humanity.

The Eucharistic Prayer, the heart of the Liturgy of the Eucharist, unfolds like a sacred symphony, each word and gesture infused with profound meaning and significance. As the priest recites the ancient words of consecration, the bread and wine are transformed into the body and blood of Christ, the living presence of our Savior made manifest on the altar. In this miraculous moment of transubstantiation, the boundaries between the earthly and the divine dissolve, and the faithful are invited to partake in the banquet of salvation.

The Communion Rite, the culmination of the Liturgy of the Eucharist, beckons the faithful to approach the altar with hearts full of reverence and humility. As the priest offers the consecrated host to each communicant, the faithful are invited to receive the body of Christ with faith and devotion, uniting themselves more closely to the divine mystery of salvation. In this sacred exchange of love, the communion of saints is made manifest, and the bonds of fellowship and unity are strengthened among the people of God.

In the final moments of the Liturgy of the Eucharist, the faithful are sent forth into the world, nourished and strengthened by the divine presence of Christ. As they carry the light of the Eucharist within their hearts, they are empowered to bear witness to the transformative power of God's love in their daily lives. The sacred ritual of the Liturgy of the Eucharist serves as a beacon of hope and renewal, guiding the faithful on their journey of faith and drawing them ever closer to the heart of God.

In essence, the Liturgy of the Eucharist is not merely a ritualistic observance but a profound encounter with the living God. It is a sacrament of love, a testament to the enduring presence of Christ in the midst of his people. As we partake in this sacred mystery, may our hearts be opened to the boundless depths of God's mercy and grace, and may we be transformed by the power of his love now and forevermore. Amen.

6

Sunday Readings and Reflections

Every Sunday, as Catholics gather to celebrate the Eucharist, they immerse themselves in the sacred scriptures through the readings carefully chosen for that day. In this section of the St. Joseph Sunday and Daily Missal Hymnal and Prayer-book 2024, we delve into the profound significance of these Sunday readings, offering insightful reflections to enrich the spiritual journey of every believer.

1. The Liturgy of the Word: A Divine Encounter

As the faithful gather in churches around the world, the Liturgy of the Word unfolds, inviting them into a divine encounter with the living Word of God. The Sunday readings, meticulously selected from the Old Testament, the Psalms, the New Testament Epistles, and the Gospels, form the cornerstone of this sacred encounter.

2. Unveiling the Treasure of Sacred Scriptures

Each Sunday, the readings presented to the faithful are not mere words on a page but living expressions of God's eternal truth and boundless love. Through insightful commentary and spiritual guidance, we unravel the layers of meaning embedded within these timeless texts, inviting readers to explore the depths of divine revelation.

3. Journeying Through Salvation History

From the creation narrative to the culmination of salvation in Christ, the Sunday readings trace the arc of salvation history, inviting believers to journey alongside the patriarchs, prophets, apostles, and saints of old. Through their struggles and tri- umphs, we discover echoes of our own spiritual journey and find solace in the enduring faithfulness of God.

4. The Gospel: Good News for Today

At the heart of the Sunday liturgy lies the proclamation of the Gospel, the good news of Jesus Christ. Through compelling narratives, parables, and teachings, the Gospels offer timeless wisdom and profound insights into the person of Jesus Christ. In our reflections, we unpack the richness of the Gospel message, inviting readers to encounter Christ anew in their lives.

5. Reflecting on the Call to Discipleship

As the Word of God is proclaimed, it beckons us to respond with hearts open to conversion and renewal. Through thought-provoking reflections, we explore the implications of the Sunday readings for our daily lives, challenging readers to embrace the call to discipleship and live out their faith with authenticity and zeal.

6. Finding Hope and Encouragement

In a world marked by uncertainty and turmoil, the Sunday

readings offer a beacon of hope and encouragement to all who seek solace in the midst of life's storms. Through stories of faith, perseverance, and redemption, we discover that God's grace is ever-present, sustaining us in times of trial and guiding us along the path of righteousness.

7. Cultivating a Spirit of Contemplation

In the hustle and bustle of modern life, the Sunday liturgy invites us to pause, reflect, and enter into a spirit of contemplation. Through meditative insights and practical reflections, we create space for the Holy Spirit to speak to our hearts, illuminating the sacred mysteries hidden within the scriptures and drawing us closer to the heart of God.

8. Nourishing the Soul with Sacred Truths

As we meditate on the Sunday readings, we are nourished by the timeless truths contained within the sacred scriptures. From the promise of salvation to the challenge of discipleship, each reading speaks to the deepest longings of the human heart, offering comfort, guidance, and inspiration for the journey ahead.

9. Embracing the Transformative Power of God's Word

Ultimately, the Sunday readings are not meant to simply inform but to transform, renewing our minds and hearts in the image of Christ. Through prayerful reflection and attentive listening, we open ourselves to the transformative power of God's Word, allowing it to penetrate the depths of our being and lead us ever closer to experiencing the richness of life in Christ.

In this section of the St. Joseph Sunday and Daily Missal Hymnal and Prayerbook 2024, we invite you to embark on a spiritual journey through the sacred scriptures, allowing the timeless truths of God's Word to illuminate your path and guide you in the way of holiness. As you engage with the Sunday readings and reflections presented here, may you encounter the living God and experience the fullness of His love and mercy in your life.

III

Daily Missal

Throughout history, the Catholic Church has fostered a rich tapestry of prayer practices, each offering unique ways to connect with God and nourish our spiritual lives

7

Morning Prayer

The quiet hush of the morning, a canvas yet untouched by the day's bustle. It's in this sacred space that many Catholics begin their day with Morning Prayer, a beautiful tapestry woven from scripture, psalms, and prayers. This practice, often referred to as Lauds, is an invitation to greet the rising sun, both literally and metaphorically, by acknowledging God's presence in our lives and surrendering the day to His will.

But what exactly does Morning Prayer entail? Let's delve into its rich tapestry, one after the other

1. The Invitatory:

The day begins with an **opening invitation**, a simple yet profound verse that sets the tone for prayer. It's like a gentle nudge, reminding us to turn our hearts and minds towards **God**. An example might be:

"O God, make speed to save me! O Lord, make haste to help me!" (Psalm 70:1).

2. Hymn:

Following the invitation, a **hymn of praise** often fills the air. These hymns, rich in tradition and melody, **lift our hearts and voices** in joyful adoration of God. They express our **gratitude** for the gift of a new day and remind us of His faithfulness and love.

3. Psalmody:

The Psalms, the very **prayers of God's people** throughout history, form the heart of Morning Prayer. Each day, specific psalms are chosen based on the liturgical season or feast day. As we recite or sing these ancient verses, we connect with **generations of believers** who have found solace and strength in the same words.

4. Scripture Reading:

A brief passage from Scripture is offered next, a seed of **God's word** planted in the fertile soil of our hearts. This reading provides guidance, inspiration, and challenges as we navigate the day ahead.

5. Canticle:

Following the Scripture reading, a **canticle**, a more poetic and song-like excerpt from the Bible, is often included. These canticles, such as the **Song of Mary (Magnificat)** or the **Song of Zechariah (Benedictus)**, offer a joyful and personal response
to God's presence in our lives.

6. Intercessions:

With hearts warmed by scripture and song, we now turn to **intercession**. This is a time to **lift up our prayers** for ourselves, our loved ones, the world, and the Church. We **petition God for His guidance, strength, and mercy,** carrying the burdens of others in our hearts.

7. The Lord's Prayer:

The **universal prayer** taught by Jesus himself, the **Our Father,** unites us with all believers across time and space. As we recite these familiar words, we are reminded of our **relationship with God as our Father** and our **belonging to a global family of faith.**

8. Concluding Prayer:

Finally, a **concluding prayer** brings Morning Prayer to a close. This prayer **summarizes the themes** explored throughout the service and **asks for God's continued presence** throughout the day.

Beyond the Structure:

Morning Prayer is more than just a collection of prayers; it's an intentional encounter with the divine. It's a commitment to starting our day centered on God, seeking His guidance and offering our gratitude. As we weave this practice into the fabric of our lives, we cultivate a deeper relationship with God, allowing His light to illuminate and guide our every step.

Remember, dear reader, Morning Prayer is not a rigid formula, but a **flexible framework** for encountering God. Feel free to **Adapt it to your own pace and preferences.** Whether you pray alone in the quiet of your home or join a community for shared prayer, allow Morning Prayer to be the **sacred space** where you **Greet the day with God** and **find strength for the journey ahead.**

8

Midday Reflections

The midday sun casts long shadows, marking the turning point of the day. Midst the whirlwind of work, errands, and daily obligations, a gentle nudge beckons us – a call to pause, reflect, and reconnect. This, dear reader, is the essence of Midday Reflections.

More than just a break in the day, Midday Reflections offer a **sacred space** to **recenter ourselves** and **reconnect with the divine.** It's a **moment of quiet contemplation,** a **chance to breathe** and allow **God's grace to permeate our busy lives.**

But how do we cultivate this practice in the midst of our hectic schedules? Here's a glimpse into the **rich tapestry** of Midday Reflections:

1. Finding Your Sanctuary:
The first step is carving out a **sacred space**, even if it's just a few stolen moments in a quiet corner of your office, a park bench bathed in sunlight, or the serene sanctuary of your own

home. This space, however temporary, becomes your **personal haven** for encountering the divine.

2. The Call to Silence:

In our world of constant noise and distractions, **silence becomes a precious commodity**. As you settle into your chosen space, **mute the external noise** and **allow the inner chatter to subside**. This intentional stillness creates the fertile ground where **God's voice can be heard**.

3. Reflecting on the Word:

Open your **Bible** or a **devotional book** and choose a short passage that resonates with you. Perhaps it's a verse that speaks to a current challenge you're facing, or a passage that offers comfort and inspiration. **Read the words slowly, savor their meaning,** and **allow them to wash over your heart and mind**.

4. Engaging in Prayer:

With the Scripture's message fresh in your mind, **turn your heart towards God in prayer**. This can be a **formal prayer** like the **Our Father** or the **Hail Mary**, or a more **spontaneous conversation** from the depths of your heart. Share your joys and concerns, **seek guidance and strength,** and **express your gratitude** for His blessings.

5. The Examen:

Consider incorporating the practice of the **Examen**, a simple yet profound tool for **self-reflection**. Briefly **review your morning** and **acknowledge the moments** where you experienced God's presence, His grace, and His guidance. **Recognize areas** where you may have fallen short and **seek forgiveness**. This practice allows you to **learn from your experiences** and **grow closer to God** throughout the day.

6. Offering of Gratitude:

In the midst of our busy lives, it's easy to overlook the countless blessings that surround us. Take a moment to **express your gratitude** for the **simple joys** – the warmth of the sun, the laughter of loved ones, the beauty of nature. **Recognizing these blessings** deepens our appreciation for God's presence in our Lives.

7. A Renewed Resolve:

As you conclude your Midday Reflections, allow the experience to **reinvigorate your spirit**. With a **renewed sense of purpose** and **commitment to God's will**, you step back into the world, **carrying the peace and strength** gleaned from your sacred pause.

Remember, dear reader, Midday Reflections are not about achieving perfection. They are about **cultivating a habit** of **intentionally turning towards God** throughout the day. Even a few stolen moments can make a world of difference, **replenishing your spirit** and **guiding your steps** as you navigate the remainder of your journey.

So, the next time the midday sun beckons, take a pause, **find your sanctuary,** and **allow yourself to be enveloped in the peace and presence of God.** You might just be surprised at the **renewed strength and clarity** that awaits you on the other side of this sacred pause.

9

Evening Vespers

As the sun dips below the horizon, painting the sky in hues of orange and gold, the Church gathers for **Evening Vespers**, also known as **Evening Prayer**. This ancient practice, steeped in tradition and rich symbolism, offers a beautiful way to **conclude the day** by **giving thanks for God's blessings** and **surrendering our burdens to His care.**

Imagine yourself nestled in the quiet embrace of a church, the gentle flicker of candlelight illuminating the faces of fellow believers. As the opening **Invitatory** rings out, a simple yet profound verse like **"O God, come to my assistance! O Lord, make haste to help me!"** (Psalm 70:1), it serves as a gentle nudge, reminding us to **turn our hearts and minds towards God** after the day's activities.

The **hymn** that follows, often filled with poignant lyrics and soothing melodies, acts as a **bridge between the world we leave behind and the sacred space we enter.** It's a time to **lift our voices in praise,** expressing **gratitude for the day's blessings** and acknowledging God's **unwavering presence** in our lives.

The heart of Vespers lies in the **Psalmody,** where we encounter the timeless **prayers of God's people** throughout history. Each day, specific psalms are chosen based on the liturgical season or feast day. As we **recite or sing these ancient verses,** we **connect with generations of believers** who have found solace and strength in the same words. These psalms, filled with expressions of **praise, lament, and petition,** offer a **mirror to our own emotions** and provide a **language for our deepest yearnings.**

Following the Psalms, a **brief passage from Scripture** is offered, a **beacon of light** guiding us through the coming night. This reading, like a **seed planted in fertile soil,** provides **inspiration and reflection** as we prepare for rest and contemplate the day's experiences.

Next comes the **Canticle,** a more **poetic and song-like excerpt from the Bible.** Often, the **Magnificat** (Song of Mary) or the **Nunc Dimittis** (Song of Simeon) are chosen, offering a **personal and joyful response** to God's presence and action in our lives. These canticles, filled with **emotion and imagery,** invite us to **sing our own song of praise and thanksgiving.**

With hearts warmed by scripture and song, we now turn to **intercession.** This is a time to **lift up our prayers** for ourselves, our loved ones, the world, and the Church. We **petition God** for His guidance, strength, and mercy, carrying the burdens of others in our hearts. As we intercede for those in need, we become instruments of compassion and love, extending God's grace to the world around us.

The universal prayer, the Our Father, unites us in a moment of shared humanity and faith. As we recite these familiar words, we are reminded of our relationship with God as our Father and our belonging to a global family of believers. This shared prayer transcends individual differences, fostering a sense of unity and connection as we entrust ourselves to God's loving care.

Finally, a concluding prayer brings Evening Vespers to a close. This prayer summarizes the themes explored throughout the service and asks for God's continued presence throughout the night. It's a gentle surrender, entrusting ourselves to God's watchful care as we prepare for sleep and the uncertainties of tomorrow.

Beyond the Structure:
   Evening Vespers is more than just a collection of prayers; it's a ritual of letting go and embracing God's presence. It's a moment of quiet reflection, allowing us to process the day's experiences and find solace in God's love. As we weave this practice into the fabric of our lives, we cultivate a sense of peace and gratitude, allowing the day's burdens to fade as we surrender to God's loving embrace.

Remember, dear reader, Evening Vespers is not a rigid for-mula, but a flexible framework for encountering God. Feel free to **adapt it to your own pace and preferences**. Whether you pray alone in the quiet of your home or join a community for shared prayer, allow Evening Vespers to be the **sacred space** where you conclude your day with God and **find peace for the night ahead.**

10

Nighttime Prayers

As the sun dips below the horizon, painting the sky in hues of orange and lavender, a natural hush descends upon the world. It's in this tranquil space, nestled between the fading light and the promise of a new dawn, that many Catholics find solace and strength in Nighttime Prayers. These prayers, often referred to as Compline or Night Prayer, are an invitation to surrender the day to God and embrace the peace of the night.

Just like Morning Prayer, Nighttime Prayers offer a beautiful tapestry woven from scripture, psalms, and prayers. Let's delve into the rich threads that make up this sacred practice:

1. The Invitatory:
Similar to Morning Prayer, Nighttime Prayers begin with an **opening invitation**, a simple yet profound verse that sets the tone for reflection and gratitude. This verse might be:

"Keep this night, O Lord, holy without sin. May your angels guard me." (Antiphon from Compline).

2. Hymn:

A soothing **hymn**, often filled with imagery of peace and rest, fills the air next. These hymns act as a **balm to the soul**, inviting us to **release the anxieties** of the day and **embrace the quietude of the night.**

3. Examination of Conscience:

Nighttime Prayers offer a unique opportunity for **introspection and reflection.** Through an **examination of conscience,** we are invited to **gently review our day,** acknowledging our shortcomings and seeking forgiveness. This practice is not about self-flagellation, but rather a **compassionate exploration** That allows us to **learn and grow** from our experiences.

4. Psalmody:

Just as in Morning Prayer, **psalms** form the heart of Nighttime Prayers. Specific psalms chosen for their themes of **gratitude, forgiveness, and trust** in God's providence guide our reflec- tion. As we recite or sing these ancient verses, we find **solace and comfort** in the timeless words that have resonated with countless believers for centuries.

5. Scripture Reading:

A **brief passage from Scripture** is offered next, a **beacon of light** guiding us through the darkness of night. This reading often speaks of **hope, peace, and God's enduring love,** offering a comforting reminder of His presence in our lives, even as we sleep.

6. Canticle:

Following the Scripture reading, a **canticle,** often the **Song of**

Simeon (Nunc Dimittis), is included. This canticle expresses a sense of **peace and contentment** as we surrender the day and prepare for sleep.

7. Intercessions:

With hearts quieted by reflection and scripture, we turn to intercession. This is a time to **lift up our prayers** for ourselves, our loved ones, the world, and the Church. We **petition God for His protection, guidance, and blessings** as we entrust ourselves and others to His loving care.

8. The Lord's Prayer:

Once again, the **universal prayer** taught by Jesus himself, the **Our Father**, unites us with all believers. As we recite these familiar words, we are reminded of our **relationship with God as our Father** and our **belonging to a global family of faith.**

9. Concluding Prayer:

A **concluding prayer** brings Nighttime Prayers to a close. This prayer **summarizes the themes** explored throughout the service and **asks for God's continued presence** throughout the night. It might be a prayer for **peaceful sleep, protection from harm, and guidance in our dreams.**

Beyond the Ritual:

Nighttime Prayers are more than just a collection of prayers; they are a **sacred ritual** that marks the **transition from the busyness of the day to the tranquility of the night.** They are an opportunity to **quiet our minds, express gratitude, and seek solace** in the presence of God. As we **weave this practice** into the fabric of our lives, we cultivate a **deeper sense of peace** and trust in God's unfailing love.

Remember, dear reader, Nighttime Prayers are not meant to be a burden, but rather a **gift of grace**. Whether you pray alone in the quiet of your bedroom or join a community for shared prayer, allow Nighttime Prayers to be the **sacred space** where you **surrender your worries, find comfort in** God's presence, and drift off to sleep with a peaceful heart.

11

Understanding the Importance of the Descent of the Holy Spirit

Fifty days after the glorious resurrection of Jesus Christ, the Church celebrates Pentecost, a pivotal moment that marks the birth of the Church and the outpouring of the Holy Spirit upon the Apostles. This event, recounted in the Acts of the Apos- tles (Acts 2:1-13), holds immense significance for Christians, shaping the very fabric of our faith.

A Descent of Power and Renewal:
The narrative of Pentecost describes a **dramatic and transformative event**. A mighty **wind** filled the upper room where the Apostles were gathered, followed by **tongues of fire** resting upon their heads. This **visible manifestation of the Holy Spirit** empowered them to speak in **foreign languages** they had never learned before. This miraculous ability served a crucial purpose: to **bridge the communication gap** between the Apostles and the diverse crowd gathered in Jerusalem for the Jewish feast of pentecost.

Significance for the Church:

The descent of the Holy Spirit marked the fulfillment of Jesus' promise to his disciples: "But the Advocate, the Holy Spirit, whom the Father will send in my name, will teach you all things and teach you all things and will remind you of everything I have said to you" (John 14:26). With the arrival of the Holy Spirit, the Apostles were equipped with the knowledge, courage, and strength necessary to carry out Christ's mission Of spreading the Gospel message to the ends of the earth.

Empowering the Disciples:

The outpouring of the Holy Spirit not only enabled the Apostles to communicate effectively but also empowered them with various gifts. These gifts, as outlined in the New Testament (1 Corinthians 12:7-11), are diverse and essential for the building up and functioning of the Church. They include wisdom, understanding, counsel, fortitude, knowledge, piety, and fear of the Lord. Additionally, the Holy Spirit bestows charisms, specific talents and abilities used for the service of the Church community.

A Continuing Presence:

The significance of Pentecost extends beyond a historical event. The Holy Spirit is not confined to that specific moment; it is a continuous and dynamic presence within the Church. Through the sacraments, prayer, and the guidance of the Church, we, as believers, can access the power and gifts of the Holy Spirit to guide our lives, strengthen our faith, and empower us to serve God and others.

The Blessings and Manifestations of the Holy Spirit

The **Holy Spirit** not only empowers us with **gifts** for service but also cultivates **fruits** within our character. These fruits, as described in Galatians 5:22-23, are the **visible manifestations** of the Holy Spirit's work in our lives. They are:

- **Love:** The foundation of all Christian virtues, expressed through compassion, kindness, and selflessness.
- **Joy:** A deep and abiding sense of happiness rooted in our relationship with God and the hope of eternal life.
- **Peace:** An inner tranquility that transcends worldly anxieties and circumstances.
- **Patience:** The ability to endure challenges and persevere through difficulties with grace and understanding.
- **Kindness:** A genuine concern for the well-being of others, expressed through acts of generosity and service.
- **Goodness:** The desire and capacity to do good, acting with integrity and moral uprightness.
- **Faithfulness:** Keeping promises, fulfilling commitments, and demonstrating unwavering loyalty to God and others.
- **Gentleness:** A spirit of meekness, humility, and understanding in our interactions with others.
- **Self-control:** The ability to manage our emotions, desires, and actions with discipline and moderation.

These **fruits** are not static achievements but rather **ongoing journeys of growth** cultivated through **prayer, reflection, and cooperation with the Holy Spirit's Wirken**. As we strive to live according to these fruits, they become **visible expressions** of our faith and **contribute to the building up of a more Christ-like world.

12

The Importance of Daily Prayer

Throughout history, the Catholic Church has fostered a rich tapestry of prayer practices, each offering unique ways to connect with God and nourish our spiritual lives. Among these practices, Morning Prayer, Midday Prayer, Evening Prayer, and Night Prayer hold a special significance, inviting us to sanctify every hour of the day and weave prayer into the fabric of our daily existence.

1. Morning Prayer: Greeting the Day with God
As the first rays of dawn paint the sky, **Morning Prayer** beckons us to **begin the day centered on God**. This practice, also known as **Lauds**, is an invitation to **acknowledge God's presence** in our lives, **surrender the day to His will**, and **seek His guidance** for the journey ahead.

Imagine the quiet hush of the morning, a canvas yet untouched by the day's bustle. In this sacred space, we open our hearts with an **opening verse**, a gentle nudge towards **turning our minds and hearts towards God**. This might be a simple yet profound verse like:

"O God, make speed to save me! O Lord, make haste to help me!" (Psalm 70:1)

As we move forward, **hymns of praise** fill the air, lifting our voices and hearts in joyful adoration. These hymns, rich in tradition and melody, express our **gratitude for the gift of a new day** and remind us of God's **faithfulness and love.**

The heart of Morning Prayer lies in the **Psalms, the very prayers of God's people** throughout history. Each day, specific psalms are chosen based on the liturgical season or feast day. As we **recite or sing these ancient verses**, we **connect with generations of believers** who have found solace and strength in the same words.

A **brief passage from Scripture** is offered next, a **seed of God's word** planted in the fertile soil of our hearts. This reading provides **guidance, inspiration, and challenges** as we navigate the day ahead.

Following the Scripture reading, a **canticle**, a more poetic and song-like excerpt from the Bible, is often included. These canticles, such as the **Song of Mary (Magnificat)** or the **Song of Zechariah (Benedictus)**, offer a **joyful and personal response** to God's presence in our lives..

With hearts warmed by scripture and song, we now turn to **intercession.** This is a time to **lift up our prayers** for ourselves, our loved ones, the world, and the Church. We **petition God for His guidance, strength, and mercy,** carrying the burdens of others in our hearts.

The **universal prayer** taught by Jesus himself, the **Our Father**, unites us with all believers across time and space. As we recite these familiar words, we are reminded of our **relationship with God as our Father** and our **belonging to a global family of faith.**

Finally, a **concluding prayer** brings Morning Prayer to a close. This prayer **summarizes the themes** explored throughout the service and **asks for God's continued presence** throughout the day..

2. Midday Prayer: A Moment of Pause in the Midst of the Day As the sun reaches its zenith, **Midday Prayer** invites us to **pause amidst the busyness** of the day and **reconnect with God.** This brief prayer service, also known as **Sext**, is a **reminder to refocus our hearts and minds on God's presence**, even in the whirlwind of daily activities.

Similar to Morning Prayer, Midday Prayer often begins with an **opening verse**, followed by a **hymn** that lifts our spirits in praise. A short **reading from Scripture** provides inspiration and guidance, and a **canticle** like the **Psalm 91** reminds us of God's protection and care. We then offer **intercessions** for ourselves and the world, and conclude with the **Our Father** and a **closing prayer.**

This brief midday pause, even amidst the demands of our schedules, serves as a **powerful reminder** that **we are not alone** in our endeavors. It allows us to **replenish our spiritual wellspring** and **face the remainder of the day with renewed focus and strength.**

3. Evening Prayer: Reflecting on the Day with Gratitude

As the day draws to a close, **Evening Prayer**, also known as **Vespers**, offers a sacred space to **reflect on the day's experiences** and **express our gratitude to God**. This practice invites us to **release the burdens** we may be carrying, **seek forgiveness for our shortcomings**, and **surrender to God's loving care** as we prepare for

IV

Liturgical Calendar

The liturgical calendar, with its ebb and flow of seasons, invites us on a profound journey of faith.

13

Advent: A Season of Hope and Preparation

As the crisp autumn air settles and the leaves begin their fiery descent, the Church enters a season unlike any other: **Advent**. This four-week period, stretching from late November to Christ- mas Eve, is a **tapestry woven with anticipation, reflection, and preparation.** It's a time to rekindle the embers of hope within our hearts and **prepare ourselves for the glorious arrival of Jesus Christ.**

But what exactly is Advent? Let's delve deeper into the rich symbolism and profound meaning embedded within this sacred season:

1. A Season of Waiting:
Fundamentally, Advent embodies the essence of anticipation. We **yearn for the arrival of the Christ child,** just as the Israelites

longed for the coming of their Messiah. This waiting, however, is not passive; it's **active and expectant.** We **engage in prayer, reflection, and acts of service,** preparing our hearts and minds to **receive the gift of Christ's presence** in a meaningful way.

2. A Season of Hope:

Advent is not merely a time of waiting; it's also a **season brimming with hope.** We **remember the promises made by God** throughout history, the prophecies foretelling the arrival of a savior. This hope **illuminates the darkness** of the winter months and **ignites a sense of anticipation** for the light and joy that Christ's birth brings.

3. A Season of Preparation:

Advent is a **season of preparation.** We **cleanse our hearts** through **prayer, fasting, and acts of charity.** We **reflect on our shortcomings** and **seek reconciliation with God and others.**

This preparation isn't just about getting ready for a festive celebration; it's about **creating space within ourselves** to fully **receive the transformative power of Christ's coming.**

4. The Four Weeks of Advent:

Each week of Advent has a distinct theme, guiding our reflection and preparation:

· **First Week: The Week of Hope:** We focus on the **prophecies** foretelling the Messiah's arrival and **cultivate a spirit of hopeful expectation.**

· **Second Week: The Week of Preparation:** We **reflect on** John the Baptist's call to repentance and **prepare our hearts for Christ's coming.**

· **Third Week: The Week of Joy:** We **rejoice in the anticipation**

54

of Christ's birth and focus on the joy He brings to the world.
· Fourth Week: The Week of Peace: We contemplate the peace that Christ offers and seek to cultivate peace within ourselves and the world.

Symbols of Advent:

· **Advent Wreath:** A circular evergreen wreath adorned with four candles, each lit on a successive Sunday of Advent, symbolizing the **growing light** as we approach Christmas.
· **Advent Calendar:** A visual reminder of the **countdown to Christmas**, often containing small treats or prayers for each day.
· **Purple Vestments:** The liturgical color used during Advent, signifying **penance, preparation, and royalty**.

Beyond the Traditions:
Advent is more than just traditions and symbols; it's an **invitation to a deeper relationship with Christ**. It's a call to slow down, reflect, and **prepare our hearts** to receive the greatest gift ever given: **the gift of God's love incarnate in Jesus christ**.

Dear reader, as you embark on this Advent journey, allow yourself to be enveloped by the spirit of hope, anticipation, and preparation. May the quiet moments of reflection and the acts of service illuminate your path. May the coming of Christ fill your heart with the joy, peace, and love that only He can bring

14

Christmas: Celebrating the Birth of Our Savior

Christmas. The very word evokes a kaleidoscope of emotions: the warmth of family gatherings, the twinkling lights adorning homes, the carols echoing through crisp winter air, and the anticipation of exchanging gifts. But midst the festive cheer, it's crucial to remember the true heart of Christmas: the celebration of the birth of Jesus Christ, our Lord and Savior.

This sacred occasion transcends the realm of mere festivity; it's a **momentous event in human history**, marking the arrival of **God's incarnate Son** into our world. As Christians, we celebrate Christmas not just with merriment, but with **reverence, gratitude, and a renewed commitment to faith.**

Let us delve deeper into the significance of Christmas, exploring its various facets:

1. The Nativity Story:
   The foundation of Christmas lies in the **glorious narrative**

recounted in the Gospels of Luke and Matthew. We encounter the **humility of Mary and Joseph**, their unwavering faith as they journey to Bethlehem, and the **miraculous birth of Jesus** in a humble manger. The arrival of the **Savior**, heralded by angels and witnessed by shepherds, signifies the **fulfillment of God's promise** to send a Messiah, a **beacon of hope and redemption** for humanity.

2. The Incarnation:
Christmas celebrates the **incarnation**, the **unveiling of the divine in human form.** The **Son of God**, existing eternally in perfect unity with the Father, takes on **flesh and blood,** becoming one with humanity. This act of **unfathomable love and humility** bridges the gap between God and humankind, offering us the possibility of **reconciliation and communion** with our Creator.

3. Light in the Darkness:
The birth of Jesus is often symbolized by a star, a **beacon of light piercing through the darkness.** This symbolism resonates deeply, for Christmas arrives during the darkest time of the year in the Northern Hemisphere. It reminds us that Jesus is the **light of the world**, dispelling the shadows of sin, ignorance, and despair. He brings **hope, love, and peace** into a world often throuded in darkness.

4. A Celebration of Family and Community:
Christmas, at its core, is a **celebration of family and community.** The gathering of loved ones around the table, the exchange of gifts, and the sharing of meals all foster a sense of **belonging, connection, and love.** This spirit of togetherness reflects the

universal family of God, where we are all brothers and sisters in Christ, bound by faith and love.

5. A Call to Action:

The celebration of Christmas is not merely a passive remembrance of the past; it's a **call to action.** The arrival of Jesus compels us to **embody His teachings** in our daily lives. We are called to **love one another**, to **practice compassion and forgiveness**, and to **share the light of Christ** with the world around us.

Beyond the Decorations:

As we partake in the festivities of Christmas, let us not lose sight of its profound significance. Let the twinkling lights and joyful carols serve as reminders of the **eternal light** that came into the world. Let the warmth of our gatherings inspire us to **embrace the love** that Christ so generously bestowed upon us. And let the spirit of giving motivate us to **share our blessings** with those in need, reflecting the **compassion and generosity** of our Savior.

May this Christmas be a time of **renewal, reflection, and joy** as we celebrate the birth of our Lord and embrace the message of hope, love, and peace that He brought into the world.

15

Lent: A Time of Reflection and Repentance

As the crisp air of winter gives way to the whispers of spring, the Church enters a season of quiet introspection and spiritual renewal: **Lent**. This sacred period, lasting **forty days** between Ash Wednesday and Easter Sunday, invites us to **embrace reflec- tion, repentance, and preparation** for the glorious celebration of Christ's resurrection.

But what exactly is Lent, and how can we embark on this meaningful journey? Let's delve into the heart of this holy season, exploring its core practices and the transformative potential it holds:

1. A Journey of Self-Reflection:

Lent is a time to **turn inward**, to **examine our lives** with honesty and humility. We are invited to **confront our shortcomings,** our **areas of weakness**, and the ways in which we may have strayed from the path of righteousness. This introspection can be aided by various practices:

· **Journaling:** Taking time each day to **reflect on our thoughts, feelings, and actions** can provide valuable insights into our personal struggles and areas for growth.

· **Spiritual reading:** Immersing ourselves in **faith-based texts** like scripture or the writings of saints can offer guid- ance, inspiration, and a deeper understanding of ourselves and our relationship with God.

· **Prayerful contemplation:** Dedicating quiet time for **silent reflection and prayer** allows us to **connect with God's presence** and listen for His voice in the depths of our hearts.

Through this inward journey, we gain a clearer understanding of ourselves, recognizing both our strengths and weaknesses. This self-awareness becomes the foundation for **genuine re- pentance** and **positive transformation.**

2. Embracing Repentance:

Having identified areas for improvement, Lent calls us to re-pent, to **turn away from sin** and **commit ourselves to a renewed life in Christ.** This repentance is not merely about feeling regret or guilt; it's a **proactive choice** to **mend our broken relationship** with God and **embrace a path of righteousness.**

Several practices can facilitate this process of repentance:

· **The Sacrament of Reconciliation:** Seeking **confession and forgiveness** through the Sacrament of Reconciliation allows us to **acknowledge our transgressions** and receive God's grace and mercy.

61

· **Acts of penance:** Engaging in **self-denial** or **acts of service** can serve as outward expressions of our inward commitment to change. These acts, while not meant to be punitive, can help us **realign our priorities** and **cultivate a deeper sense of humility.**

· **Prayer for forgiveness:** Regularly approaching God in **sincere prayer**, acknowledging our shortcomings, and seeking His forgiveness is a powerful step towards repentance and renewal.

By embracing repentance, we **open ourselves to God's transformative grace** and **set the stage for spiritual growth.**

3. A Season of Preparation:

Lent is not just about introspection and repentance; it's also a time of **preparation** for the **joyous celebration of Easter.** As we journey through these forty days, we are invited to **prepare our hearts and minds** to fully **receive the gift of Christ's resurrection.**

This preparation can take various forms:

· **Increased prayer and devotion:** Dedicating more time to **personal prayer, scripture reading, and participation in liturgical celebrations** deepens our connection with God and fosters a spirit of anticipation for Easter.

· **Almsgiving:** Sharing our blessings with those in need through **acts of charity and generosity** reflects Christ's teachings on love and compassion and prepares our hearts for the celebration of His ultimate sacrifice.

· **Fasting and abstinence:** While not mandatory for all, **fasting** (reducing food intake) and **abstinence** (giving up something enjoyable) can serve as **disciplines** that help us **focus on our spiritual growth** and **develop self-control**.

By actively engaging in these practices of preparation, we **create space within ourselves** to **fully appreciate** the **significance of Easter** and **embrace the transformative power of Christ's resurrection**.

Lent, a Season of Transformation:

Lent is not merely a somber period on the Christian calendar; it's a **season of immense potential** for **personal growth, spiritual renewal, and a deeper connection with God.** By embracing **reflection, repentance, and preparation,** we embark on a **transformative journey** that culminates in the **joyous celebration of Easter** and a renewed commitment to living a Life **inspired by Christ's love and teachings.**

Remember, dear reader, this Lenten season is a **personal invitation** from God to **draw closer to Him**. Embrace the journey with an open heart and a willingness to grow, and allow yourself to be **transformed by the power of His love and grace.**

16

Easter: Rejoicing in the Resurrection

The air hums with anticipation, a collective breath held in the quiet hush before the storm. The weight of the past week, the somber remembrance of Christ's suffering and sacrifice, hangs heavy in the hearts of believers. But then, a dawning light pierces the darkness, a whisper of hope carried on the gentle breeze. Easter Sunday has arrived, and with it, a joyous explosion of faith that reverberates through every fiber of our being.

This is the day we celebrate the **triumph of life over death**, the **victory of light over darkness**. It's a day etched in the very fabric of Christianity, a cornerstone of our belief system, and a **festival of unbridled joy**. But what exactly does Easter signify, and how do we, as Catholics, celebrate this momentous occasion?

1. The Resurrection Narrative:

At the heart of Easter lies the **transformative story** of Jesus' resurrection from the dead. The Gospels recount how, after enduring the excruciating agony of the crucifixion and being laid to rest in a tomb, Jesus miraculously rose again on the third day. This event, a **transcendent act of divine power**, shattered the shackles of death and offered **irrefutable proof of God's love and promise of eternal life.**

2. From Sorrow to Celebration:

The days leading up to Easter are marked by **reflection and remembrance.** We participate in **HolyWeek** observances, commemorating the events that unfolded before the crucifixion, including **Palm Sunday, Maundy Thursday,** and **Good Friday.** These somber rituals allow us to **contemplate the depths of christ's sacrifice** and the profound impact it has on our lives.

However, with the dawning of Easter Sunday, the mood shifts dramatically. **Sorrow transforms into exuberant joy,** as we celebrate the ultimate victory of good over evil. Churches come alive with the **joyous sounds of hymns and music,** while vibrant colors replace the muted tones of the previous week.

3. Easter Traditions:

Easter celebrations are steeped in rich **traditions** that have been passed down through generations. These traditions, both **symbolic and celebratory,** serve to **deepen our connection to the faith** and create lasting memories.

 • **TheEasterVigil:** HeldonHolySaturdaynight,thissolemn yet joyous ceremony marks the official beginning of Easter celebrations. It features the **lighting of the Easter fire,** symbolizing the **triumph of light over darkness,** and the **renewal of baptismal vows.**
 ·**The Easter Egg:** A universal symbol of Easter, the Easter egg

represents **new life and rebirth**. Traditionally decorated in vibrant colors and intricate patterns, they serve as a reminder of the **resurrection** and the **promise of new beginnings.**

· **The Easter Feast:** Following Easter Sunday Mass, families and communities gather for a joyous Easter feast. This shared meal signifies **fellowship, unity, and the celebration of new life.**

4. The Significance of Easter:

The significance of Easter extends far beyond the confines of religious observance. It is a **universal message of hope** that transcends cultural and religious boundaries. It speaks to the **human yearning for meaning, purpose, and the possibility of overcoming even the most daunting challenges.**

Easter reminds us that **darkness is not permanent,** that **suffering can be transformed,** and that **even in the face of death, there is hope for renewal and eternal life.** It is a **powerful mes- sage** that resonates deeply within us, offering solace, strength, and a renewed sense of purpose in our lives.

5. A Call to Action:

The joy of Easter is not meant to be a fleeting experience confined to a single day. It is a **call to action,** an invitation to **embrace the transformative power of Christ's resurrection** in our daily lives. We are called to:

· **Live with hope and optimism:** Easter reminds us that even in the face of adversity, there is always hope for a brighter future. We are called to carry this message of hope into the world, inspiring others and fostering a sense of optimism in the face of challenges.

· **Spread love and compassion:** Just as Christ's love encompassed all, we are called to extend love and compassion
to those around us. This can take many forms, from acts of kindness towards strangers to acts of forgiveness and reconciliation within our own families and communities.

· **Sharethemessageoffaith:** Easterisapowerfultestament to the transformative power of faith. We are called to share this message with others, not through forceful conversion, but through our actions, our words, and the way we live our lives.

By embracing the spirit of Easter and embodying its message in our daily lives, we become living testaments to the **triumph of hope, love, and faith.** We become beacons of light, illuminating the world with the transformative power of Christ's resurrec- tion.

17

Ordinary Time: Embracing the Mission of Christ

The liturgical calendar, with its ebb and flow of seasons, invites us on a profound journey of faith. While seasons like Advent and Lent hold a distinct focus on preparation and penance, the vast expanse of **Ordinary Time**, encompassing over thirty Sundays, might seem, at first glance, less remarkable. Yet, within this seemingly ordinary space lies an extraordinary call: to **embrace the mission of Christ** in the everyday tapestry of our lives.

Ordinary Time, a canvas vast and vibrant, is not a time of stagnancy, but a time of ongoing transformation. It is a call to **integrate the teachings and spirit of Christ** into the very fabric of our existence, from the mundane to the momentous. It is a season where the **seeds of faith** sown in the fertile ground of our hearts during other liturgical seasons are nurtured, challenged, and encouraged to **blossom into acts of love, service, and**

compassion.

But how do we, ordinary people navigating the complexities of daily life, **embrace this extraordinary call**? Let us delve deeper into the essence of Ordinary Time, exploring its significance and uncovering ways to **weave the mission of Christ** into the intricate tapestry of our days:

1. A Call to Discipleship:

Ordinary Time is not merely a passive observance; it is an **active invitation to discipleship.** We are called to **go beyond the pews** and **translate our faith into concrete action.** This discipleship manifests in various forms, from **acts of kindness towards those in need** to **standing up for justice and advocating for the marginalized.** Every encounter, every decision, becomes an opportunity to **embody the teachings of christ** and **contribute to the building of His Kingdom.**

2. The Power of the Gospel:

The **gospel readings** during Ordinary Time serve as a **guiding light** on this journey of discipleship. Each Sunday, we encounter **stories, parables, and teachings** that challenge us to **reflect on our own lives** and **align our actions with Christ's message.** As we delve into these scriptures, we are invited to **confront our biases, embrace forgiveness, cultivate compassion, and live** with authenticity.

3. The Sacraments: Nourishing the Journey:

The **sacraments,** particularly the **Eucharist,** serve as **nourishment** for our spiritual growth during Ordinary Time. By **participating actively in the Mass** and **receiving Holy Communion,** we **strengthen our connection with Christ** and **draw upon His grace** to navigate the challenges and opportunities of daily life. The Eucharist becomes the **fuel** that empowers us to **live out the mission of Christ** with greater zeal and commitment.

4. A Community of Faith:

We aren't meant to journey through discipleship on our own. The **Church,** a **community of believers,** provides **support, encouragement, and guidance** on our journey. Through fellow- ship, prayer, and shared service, we learn from one another, uplift each other in times of need, and collectively strive to embody Christ's message in the world.

5. Living the Mission in the Ordinary:

The beauty of Ordinary Time lies in the realization that the **mission of Christ** does not require extraordinary feats. It is **woven into the fabric of our everyday lives,** waiting to be embraced in the **seemingly mundane moments.** A **smile offered to a stranger, a helping hand extended to a neighbor, a word of encouragement spoken with kindness** – these seemingly ordinary acts, when done with love and compassion, become **powerful expressions of Christ's love** in the world.

Ordinary Time, then, is a season of transformation, a time to step into the extraordinary by embracing the ordinary. It is a call to live the Gospel not just on Sundays, but every single day, transforming our homes, workplaces, and communities into testaments to the love and compassion of Christ. As we commit ourselves to this ongoing journey, we become instruments of God's grace, spreading light and hope in a world that yearns for it most.

Remember, dear reader, **you are not an insignificant speck in the grand scheme of things**. You are a **vital thread** in the tapestry of God's love, called to **make a difference**, one ordinary act at a time. **Embrace the call of Ordinary Time, and allow the extraordinary mission of Christ to blossom** within you and through you.

V

Devotion and prayers

Life is a rich tapestry crafted from strands of joy and sorrow, triumph and tribulation. In the midst of its intricate design, moments arise where our hearts yearn for something more, a whisper on the wind carrying a specific plea, a longing for solace or intervention

18

The Rosary: A Pathway to Peace.

The Rosary. More than just a string of beads, it's a **mystical pathway** leading us to the very heart of God. Within its simple structure lies a **profound beauty**, a **rich tapestry** woven from **prayer, meditation, and contemplation**. For centuries, the Rosary has been a **source of solace, strength, and peace** for countless Catholics, offering a **guiding light** through life's joys and sorrows.

But what exactly is the Rosary, and how can it lead us to peace? Let's embark on a journey through its **sacred mysteries**, pausing to savor the **treasures** hidden within each bead:

1.The gesture of making the Sign of the Cross and reciting the Apostles' Creed.

Our journey begins with the familiar **Sign of the Cross**, a gesture that marks the beginning of our prayer and reminds us of the saving power of Christ's sacrifice. We then recite the **Apostles' Creed**, a concise summary of our faith, grounding ourselves in the core **beliefs** that unite us as Catholics.

2. The Opening Prayer:

With hearts prepared, we offer an **opening prayer**, invoking the intercession of the Blessed Virgin Mary and seeking her guidance as we contemplate the mysteries of the Rosary.

3. The Five Decades:

The heart of the Rosary lies in its **five decades**, each representing a **specific event** in the lives of Jesus and Mary. As we meditate on these mysteries, we are **transported** back in time, **witnessing** the pivotal moments of salvation history unfold:

• **The Joyful Mysteries:** These mysteries focus on the **incarnation and early life** of Jesus, from the Annunciation to the Finding in the Temple. As we contemplate these joyful events, we are filled with **hope, wonder, and gratitude** for the gift of God's Son.

• **The Luminous Mysteries:** Added by Pope John Paul II in 2002, these mysteries highlight the **public ministry** of Jesus, from the Baptism in the Jordan to the Last Supper. By meditating on these luminous mysteries, we gain a deeper understanding of **Jesus' teachings and mission.**

• **The Sorrowful Mysteries:** These mysteries center on the **Passion and death** of Jesus, from the Agony in the Garden to the Crucifixion and Burial. As we contemplate these sorrowful events, we are filled with **compassion, empathy, and a renewed appreciation** for the depth of Christ's love and sacrifice.

• **The Glorious Mysteries:** These mysteries celebrate the

urrection and glorification of Jesus, from the Resurrection to the Coronation of Mary in Heaven. By meditating on these glorious mysteries, we are filled with **faith, hope, and anticipation** for our own eternal life in Christ.

4. The Pater Noster, Hail Mary, and Glory Be:

As we contemplate each mystery, we recite a series of prayers: the **Our Father**, the **Hail Mary**, and the **Glory Be**. These familiar prayers, repeated throughout the Rosary, serve as a **meditative rhythm**, helping us to **focus on the mysteries** and **deepen our connection** with God and Mary.

5. The Fatima Prayer:

Following the five decades, many Catholics choose to recite the **Fatima Prayer**, a prayer for peace taught by the Blessed Virgin Mary to three shepherd children in Fatima, Portugal. This prayer serves as a **powerful reminder** of our need for **peace** In our own lives and in the world.

6. The Concluding Prayer:

Finally, the Rosary concludes with a **closing prayer**, summarizing the intentions offered throughout the meditation and expressing our **gratitude** for the time spent in prayer.

The Fruits of the Rosary:

The Rosary is not merely a passive recitation of prayers; it's an **active engagement** with the mysteries of our faith. As we **contemplate** these mysteries, we are **transformed** by them. The Rosary can bear many fruits in our lives, including:

• **Deeper faith:** By meditating on the life of Christ, our faith is **strengthened and deepened.**

• **IncreasedloveforGodandMary:** Aswecontemplatetheir love and sacrifice, our own love for them grows deeper.

• **Greater peace and serenity:** The repetitive nature of the Rosary can be **calming and meditative,** fostering a sense of inner peace.

• **Growth in virtue:** By reflecting on the mysteries, we are inspired to **live more Christ-like lives.**

• **Astrongersenseofcommunity:** PrayingtheRosary,either individually or with others, fosters a sense of **belonging and connection** to the wider Catholic community.

A Pathway to Peace:

In today's world, filled with uncertainty and turmoil, the Rosary offers a **beacon of hope and a pathway to peace.**

19

Stations of the Cross: Walking with Christ in His Passion

The Stations of the Cross, also known as the Way of the Cross or Via Crucis, is a powerful devotional practice that invites us to contemplate the final hours of Jesus' life on earth. It's a journey of compassion as we walk alongside Christ, witnessing his suffering and ultimately, his sacrifice.

Fourteen distinct moments, depicted in artwork or marked by simple stations, guide our reflection. Each station offers a **glimpse into the physical and emotional agony** Jesus endured, but also reveals his **unwavering love, courage, and unwavering faith.**

Let us embark on this sacred journey together, pausing at each station to **ponder its significance** and **draw inspiration** from Christ's example:

1. Jesus is Condemned to Death:
Pontius Pilate, the Roman governor, succumbs to pressure

and **condemns Jesus to death** despite finding no guilt in him. This station reminds us of the **injustice** Jesus faced and the **power of the crowd** to sway even those in authority.

2. Jesus Accepts His Cross:

Taking up the heavy wooden cross, Jesus **embraces his fate** with **humility and obedience**. This act of acceptance signifies his **willingness to suffer** for the sake of humanity.

3. Jesus Falls the First Time:

The weight of the cross, both physical and emotional, takes its toll. Jesus **falls beneath its burden**, highlighting his **humanity and vulnerability**. Yet, he rises again, demonstrating his **resilience and determination**.

4. Jesus Meets His Mother:

Midst the chaos and cruelty, a tender moment unfolds. Jesus **encounters his mother, Mary**, their eyes meeting in a silent exchange of love and sorrow. This station reminds us of the **unbreakable bond** between mother and child, even in the face of immense suffering.

5. Simon of Cyrene Helps Carry the Cross:

Struggling with the weight of the cross, Jesus is **aided by Simon of Cyrene**. This act of **compassion**, though seemingly small, offers a glimmer of **human kindness** amidst the darkness.

6. Veronica Wipes the Face of Jesus:

A woman named Veronica, moved by compassion, **wipes the sweat and blood from Jesus' face**. This act of **tenderness** serves as a reminder of the **importance of showing compassion** to those suffering.

7. Jesus Falls the Second Time:

The weight of the cross proves too much, and Jesus **falls again**. This repeated fall underscores the **intensity of his physical suffering** and the **immense burden he carries for our sake.**

8. Jesus Meets the Women of Jerusalem:

Witnessing Jesus' suffering, the women of Jerusalem **weep for him.** This station reminds us of the **power of empathy** and the **universal nature of human compassion**.

9. Jesus Falls the Third Time:

Exhausted and drained, Jesus **falls for the third time.** This final fall signifies the **depth of his physical and emotional suffering** as he nears the end of his journey.

10. Jesus is Stripped of His Garments:

Before the crucifixion, Jesus is **stripped of his garments,** leaving him **exposed and vulnerable.** This act of humiliation serves as a stark reminder of his **complete surrender** to his fate.

11. Jesus is Nailed to the Cross:

The most agonizing moment arrives as Jesus is **nailed to the cross**. This act of violence underscores the **cruelty** he endured and the **immensity of his sacrifice**.

12. Jesus Dies on the Cross:

After enduring hours of physical and emotional torment, Jesus **utters his final words** and **breathes his last.** This station marks the **culmination of his suffering** and the completion of his earthly ministry.

13. Jesus is Taken Down from the Cross:

With his sacrifice complete, Jesus' body is **carefully lowered from the cross**. This act signifies the **end of his physical suffering** and the beginning of the **preparation for his burial**.

14. Jesus is Laid in the Tomb:

Jesus' body is **placed in a tomb**, marking the **conclusion of the Way of the Cross**. However, this is not the end of the story. This station serves as a **reminder of the promise of resurrection** and the hope for eternal life.

Walking with Christ:

As we contemplate each station, we are invited to **not just observe, but to participate**. We **imagine ourselves present** at each scene, **feeling the emotions** of the characters, and **pondering the significance** of each event.

The Stations of the Cross is not meant to be a morbid exercise, but rather a **journey of faith and transformation**. By **walking with Christ**

20

Novenas: Praying with Perseverance and Faith

In the tapestry of Catholic traditions, few practices hold the power to deepen our connection with the divine quite like the novena. This devotional act, rooted in the word "novem" meaning nine, signifies a nine-day period of dedicated prayer, a focused journey towards a specific intention or in preparation for a special feast day.

But what exactly is a novena, and how can it enrich our spiritual lives? Let'sembarkonapilgrimagethroughitsessence, exploring each step with the reverence it deserves:

1. Choosing Your Intention:

The heart of a novena lies in **setting a clear intention**. This could be a personal plea for guidance, strength, or healing. Perhaps you yearn for deeper faith, seek intercession for a loved one, or desire to prepare your heart for a significant feast day. Whatever your purpose, **approach it with sincerity and openness**.

2. Selecting Your Novena:

A vast array of novenas exists, each catering to specific needs and devotions. Popular choices include novenas to **Sacred Heart of Jesus, Our Lady of Guadalupe,** or **Saint Jude,** the patron saint of lost causes. You can also find novenas dedicated to **virtues** like patience, courage, or wisdom. Explore various resources, seeking a novena that resonates with your intention and spiritual inclinations.

3. Setting the Stage:

Just as we prepare our physical space for a guest, **create a sacred atmosphere** for your novena. Choose a quiet corner in your home, perhaps adorned with a crucifix, religious image, or a lit candle. This designated space becomes a **sanctuary for focused prayer and reflection.**

4. Embracing the Rhythm:

The essence of a novena lies in its **perseverance.** Dedicate yourself to **praying daily for nine consecutive days.** Consistency fosters **deeper reflection** and allows your intention to take root within your heart. Choose a time that fits your schedule, whether it's the quiet of the morning or the stillness of the evening.

5. The Structure of Prayer:

Each day of your novena typically follows a similar structure. It often begins with an **opening prayer,** invoking the Holy Spirit's guidance and setting the tone for your reflection. This is followed by the **specific prayers** associated with your chosen novena, which may include scripture readings, meditations, and intercessions. Many novenas conclude with the **Our Father,** the Hail Mary, and a **closing prayer**, offering thanks and entrusting your intention to God's loving care.

6. Personalizing Your Prayer:

While the framework of a novena provides structure, remember that **true prayer is a personal conversation with the divine**. Don't hesitate to **weave your own thoughts and feelings** into the prescribed prayers. Share your joys, anxieties, and hopes with God, allowing your heart to speak freely.

7. Beyond the Nine Days:

The culmination of the nine-day novena doesn't signify the end of your connection with your chosen intention. Allow the **seeds of faith and perseverance** sown during your novena to continue flourishing in your life. Integrate the lessons learned and the prayers offered into your daily spiritual practice.

The Power of Perseverance:

The beauty of the novena lies not just in the specific prayers offered, but in the **act of dedicated prayer** itself. It's a testament to our **faith, perseverance, and trust in God's loving presence**. As we faithfully commit to these nine days of prayer, we **open ourselves to deeper transformation**, allowing God's grace to work within us and guide us on our spiritual journey.

Remember, dear reader, a novena is not a magical formula, but a sacred space for cultivating your relationship with God. Approach it with an open heart, a spirit of dedication, and the unwavering belief that even the smallest prayers, offered with perseverance, can blossom into miracles of faith and hope.

21

Prayers for Special Intentions: Whispers Heard in the Stillness

Life is a rich tapestry crafted from strands of joy and sorrow, triumph and tribulation. In the midst of its intricate design, moments arise where our hearts yearn for something more, a whisper on the wind carrying a specific plea, a longing for solace or intervention. These are the moments for **prayers for special intentions**, heartfelt supplications that reach beyond the ordinary, seeking guidance, comfort, or a miraculous touch in the face of unique challenges.

1. Identifying the Need:

The first step in this sacred act is **recognizing the need** that stirs within. Is it a loved one battling illness, a weight of worry pressing down, or a yearning for direction at a crossroads? Identifying the specific concern allows us to **focus our prayer** with clarity and purpose.

2. Finding the Words:

Once the need is identified, the search for words begins. While there are many beautiful pre-written prayers for various inten- tions, sometimes the **most powerful utterances** are those born from the **depths of our own hearts**. Speak simply, honestly, and with **vulnerability**, laying bare your concerns before the Divine.

3. Scriptural Inspiration:

The **rich tapestry of scripture** offers a wealth of inspiration for crafting prayers for special intentions. Delving into passages that resonate with your specific situation can provide **comfort, guidance, and words** to articulate your needs. Perhaps it's a psalm of lament in times of sorrow, a verse of hope in moments of despair, or a passage of encouragement when facing a daunting task.

4. Intercessory Saints:

The **Catholic tradition** offers a beautiful practice of seeking the **intercession of saints**. These holy men and women, who have walked the path before us, can serve as **powerful advocates** before God. Choose a saint whose life or story resonates with your intention, and **petition their intercession** alongside your own prayer.

5. Visualization and Gratitude:

As you pray, allow yourself to **visualize** the desired outcome. See your loved one healed, the burden lifted, or the path ahead illuminated. **Gratitude**, even in the midst of difficulty, is a powerful force. Expressing thanks for the blessings already present in your life, even as you voice your specific needs, opens your heart to receive further grace.

6. Surrender and Acceptance:

Remember, dear reader, that **prayer is not about dictating outcomes** but about **communion with the Divine**. While we may hold specific desires, ultimately, we **surrender to God's will**. Trust that even in the face of unanswered prayers, His presence remains, offering strength, solace, and the unwavering assurance of His love.

7. Repetition and Perseverance:

Persistent prayer is a hallmark of faith. Don't be discouraged if your prayers seem unanswered at first. Continue to **lift your voice**, even if it's just a whisper in the stillness. Repetition, like the steady rhythm of waves against the shore, can **carve a path into the heart of the Divine**.

8. Community and Shared Prayer:

There is a **power in shared prayer**. Consider joining a **prayer group** or seeking the support of a spiritual companion to **lift up your intentions together**. The collective energy of faith and the knowledge that others are praying alongside you can be a source of immense strength and comfort.

Remember, prayers for special intentions are not mere words uttered into the void. They are **heartfelt expressions** of our deepest needs, **bridges connecting us to the Divine**, and a testament to the enduring power of faith in the face of life's challenges. As you embark on this sacred journey, may your prayers find fertile ground in the heart of God, and may you experience the profound peace and strength that comes from surrendering your burdens to His loving care.

VI

Liturgical Hymns

The tapestry of the Catholic liturgical year is woven with vibrant threads, each season bringing its own unique character and message

22

Hymns for the Liturgical Seasons

The tapestry of the Catholic liturgical year is woven with vibrant threads, each season bringing its own unique character and mes- sage. And just as the colors of the vestments change throughout the year, so too do the hymns that resonate most deeply within our hearts. These **hymns for the liturgical seasons** are not mere musical accompaniment; they are **powerful expressions of faith, guiding us through the joys and sorrows** of the Christian calendar.

Advent: A Season of Anticipation
As we enter the **season of Advent**, a hush falls over the Church, apregnant pause filled with **expectation and longing**. The hymns of this season echo this anticipation, weaving together themes of **prophecy, preparation, and hope**. We sing of the **coming Messiah**, the **promise of redemption**, and the **joyful expectation** of His birth. Hymns like **"O Come, O Come,**

Emmanuel" and "People Look East" capture the essence of this waiting period, reminding us that even in the darkness, the light of Christ is coming.

Christmas: A Celebration of Light

With the joyous arrival of **Christmas**, the Church bursts into song. Hymns of **unbridled joy and celebration** fill the air, as we **relive the wonder of the Nativity**. We sing of the **shepherds and angels**, the **star shining brightly**, and the **manger cradling the newborn King**. Carols like "**Silent Night**" and "**Joy to the World**" resonate across generations, reminding us of the In**carnation's profound gift** of hope and love.

Lent: A Time for Reflection

As we enter the **season of Lent**, the mood shifts to one of **introspection and repentance**. The hymns of this season are more subdued, inviting us to **contemplate our own shortcomings** and **seek God's forgiveness**. We sing of **sacrifice, fasting, and prayer**, echoing the forty days Jesus spent in the wilderness. Hymns like "**Lead Me, Lord, Lead Me to the Cross**" and "**Amazing Grace**" become companions on our Lenten journey, guiding us towards **renewal and spiritual growth**.

Easter: A Triumphant Explosion

The **joy of Easter** explodes into the Church with a **symphony of jubilant** hymns. We celebrate **Christ's glorious resurrection**, His **victory over death**, and the **promise of eternal life**. Hymns like "**Alleluia, Sing to Jesus!**" and "**The King Is Coming**" resonates with the triumphant spirit of the season, reminding us that the light of Christ cannot be extinguished by darkness.

Ordinary Time: A Journey of Faith

Ordinary Time, which encompasses the longest portion of the liturgical year, is a time for **growth and discipleship**. The hymns of this season focus on various aspects of the Christian life, including **faith, hope, love, service, and perseverance.** We sing of **following Christ's teachings, living out our faith in everyday life,** and **building the Kingdom of God.** Hymns like "How Great Thou Art" and "Let There Be Peace on Earth" become companions on our lifelong journey of faith, reminding usof our **commitment to God and to one another.**

Pentecost: The Gift of the Spirit

The **season of Pentecost** celebrates the **descent of the Holy Spirit** upon the Apostles, empowering them to spread the Gospel message. The hymns of this season focus on the **gifts of the Spirit,** including **wisdom, understanding, counsel, fortitude, knowledge, piety, and fear of the Lord.** We sing of the **renewal of the Church,** the **power of the Holy Spirit,** and the **mission to spread the Good News** to the ends of the earth. Hymns such as "Come, Holy Spirit" and "How Can I Keep from Singing?" encapsulate the essence of this vibrant season, prompting us to reflect on the continuous presence and influence of the Holy Spirit in our lives.

Beyond the Notes: A Symphony of Faith

The hymns of the liturgical seasons are more than just beautiful melodies; they are **expressions of the collective faith journey** of the Church throughout the year. They **guide us through moments of joy and sorrow, challenge us to grow in our faith,** and **connect us to generations of believers** who have sung these same songs before us. As we join our voices in these

95

hymns, we become part of a **symphony of faith** that resonates across time and space, **lifting our hearts and minds to God** and **deepening our connection to the Church community.**

Remember, dear reader, the hymns of the liturgical seasons are not mere entertainment, but a vital part of our faith journey. Engage with them wholeheartedly, allowing their lyrics and melodies to transport you deeper

23

Hymns for Special Occasions

The tapestry of Catholic life is woven with threads of not only liturgical seasons but also special occasions that mark moments of joy, sorrow, and significance. These occasions, from weddings and baptisms to funerals and anniversaries, are often accompanied by hymns that resonate with the emotions and themes of the day. Just as hymns enrich the liturgical year, hymns for special occasions offer a unique opportunity to express our faith, share emotions, and find solace during these significant moments.

Weddings: A Celebration of Love and Commitment

On the joyous day of a wedding, hymns become the soundtrack to a **celebration of love and commitment**. They express the **sacredness of marriage,** the **beauty of lifelong partnership,** and the **unconditional love of God.** Uplifting hymns like **"How Beautiful"** and **"The Lord's Prayer"** create a **reverent atmosphere,** while others, like **"Canticle of the Wedding"** and **"Here I Am, Lord,"** focus on the **covenant vows** and the **joys** and challenges of married life.

Baptisms: Welcoming New Life into the Faith

The baptism of a child is a joyous occasion that marks their entrance into the Christian community. Hymns sung on this special day celebrate the gift of new life, the innocence of a child, and the promise of faith. Gentle melodies and hopeful lyrics, like those found in "Holy Spirit, Gentle Dove" and "All Things Bright and Beautiful," create a warm and welcoming atmosphere, while hymns such as "One Bread, One Body" and "Go Make Disciples of All Nations" emphasize the child's inclusion in the Church family and their future role as witnesses to Christ.

Funerals: Finding Solace in Faith

During times of grief, hymns offer a source of comfort and solace for those who mourn. They express faith in eternal life, the hope of resurrection, and the peace that comes from God's love. Hymns like "Amazing Grace" and "Nearer, My God, to Thee" offer solace and strength, while others, such as "Pie Jesu" and "Eternal Rest Grant Unto Them," acknowledge the pain of loss while offering hope for the future.

Anniversaries: Celebrating Milestones of Faith

Whether celebrating the anniversary of a priest's ordination, a couple's wedding anniversary, or the dedication of a church, hymns play a significant role in marking the occasion and expressing gratitude. Hymns of praise and thanksgiving, such as "The Lord Is My Shepherd" and "How Great Thou Art," remind us of God's blessings, while others, like "For All the Saints" and "God of Grace and God of Glory," highlight the faithfulness of God and the enduring legacy of the Church.

Beyond the Melody: A Tapestry of Emotions

Hymns for special occasions are more than just musical selec- tions; they are woven into the fabric of our faith experiences, offering comfort, joy, and inspiration during significant mo- ments. They allow us to express emotions that words alone may struggle to convey and connect us to a deeper spiritual reality. As we raise our voices in song, we find solace in shared faith, celebrate milestones with gratitude, and navigate life's transitions with the enduring presence of God by our side.

Remember, dear reader, hymns for special occasions are not mere fillers, but meaningful expressions of faith. Choose them thoughtfully, allowing their lyrics and melodies to resonate with the emotions of the day and guide you on your faith journey.

24

Hymns for the Season of Pentecost: A Celebration of the Spirit's Song

The season of Pentecost, following Eastertide, bursts forth with a vibrant symphony of hymns that celebrate the descent of the Holy Spirit upon the Apostles. These hymns are not mere musical accompaniment; they are **expressions of the joy, power, and transformative presence of the Spirit** in our lives. 1. **Come, HolySpirit, Come Down:** This beloved hymn, often sung at the beginning of Pentecost celebrations, captures the essence of our longing for the Spirit's presence. The lyrics, "Come, Holy Spirit, come down as fire, come down as wind, renew our hearts within," evoke the **powerful and transformative** nature of the Spirit's Wirken.

2. **How Can I Keep from Singing?:** This joyful hymn overflows with **gratitude and praise** for the gifts of the Holy Spirit. The repeated refrain, "How can I keep from singing? My heart overflows with love," expresses the **uncontainable**

joy that comes from experiencing the Spirit's presence.

3. **Breathon Me, Breath of God:** Thiscontemplativehymn invites the Spirit to **fill us with His breath**, renewing our hearts and minds. The lyrics, "Breathe on me, Breath of God, till I am full of Thee," reflect a yearning for a **deeper connection** with the divine.

4. **Come, Creator Spirit:** This ancient hymn, dating back to the 4th century, is a powerful invocation of the Holy Spirit. It calls upon the Spirit to **enlighten our minds, inflame our hearts, and strengthen our wills.** The rich theological language of this hymn underscores the **essential role** of the Spirit in our Christian lives.

5. **Send Us Your Love:** This contemporary hymn expresses a yearning for the **Spirit's love to flow through us and into the world.** The lyrics, "Send us your love, like fire from above, to heal and unite, to set hearts alight," capture the **transformative power** of the Spirit to bring **healing, unity, Infuse love into our lives and the world surrounding us.**

6. **The Wind Upon the Face of the Deep:** This evocative hymn draws inspiration from the creation story in Genesis, where the **Spirit of God hovered over the face of the waters.** The lyrics, "The wind upon the face of the deep, stirred life from chaos, wakened from sleep," remind us that the **Spirit is the source of all creation** and continues to **breathe new life** into the world and into our hearts.

7. **Spirit of Life, Fall Fresh on Me:** This hymn expresses a **personal plea** for the Spirit's renewal. The lyrics, "Spirit of Life, fall fresh on me, melt stubborn ice and set me free," acknowledge our need for the Spirit's **transforming power** to break down barriers and **liberate us from sin and self-**

centeredness.

8. Lord,YouHaveCometoSetUsFree: Thishymncelebrates the **liberating power of the Holy Spirit**. The lyrics, "Lord, you have come to set us free, from sin and fear and slavery," remind us that the Spirit empowers us to **break free from the shackles of sin** and live in the **freedom of God's children**.

9. **One Bread, One Body**: This hymn emphasizes the **unity** that the Holy Spirit creates among believers. The lyrics, "One bread, one body, one Spirit we share, one in the Lord, in love and in prayer," celebrate the **communion** that the Spirit fosters within the Church, breaking down barriers and uniting us as one family in Christ.

10. **Sing to the Holy Spirit**: This joyful hymn concludes our exploration with a final burst of praise. The lyrics, "Sing to the Holy Spirit, sing with all your heart, sing of the love that binds us, never to depart," remind us to **continuously sing the praises** of the Holy Spirit, whose presence is the source of our **joy, hope, and transformation.**

These are just a few examples of the many hymns that enrich the season of Pentecost. As we sing these hymns, we **open ourselves to the transformative power of the Holy Spirit,** allowing Him to **renew our hearts, guide our steps, and empower us to live as instruments of His love** in the world.

25

Traditional Catholic Hymns: A Tapestry of Faith Woven in Song

The Catholic Church boasts a rich and vibrant treasury of hymns, each a sacred thread woven into the tapestry of our faith. These timeless melodies transcend generations, carrying the weight of tradition and the echoes of countless voices raised in prayer and praise. But beyond their beauty, traditional Catholic hymns hold a deeper significance, serving as powerful expressions of our beliefs, shaping our understanding of the divine, and fostering a sense of community within the Church.

1. Hymns as Expressions of Faith:

Traditional hymns are not merely musical accompaniments; they are **theological statements** set to music. They capture the essence of **dogma, scripture, and Catholic teaching**, translating complex concepts into **accessible language** that resonates with the heart. Hymns like **"Adoro Te Devote"** express profound adoration for the Eucharist, while **"O God, Our Help in Ages Past"** reminds us of God's enduring faithfulness throughout history. Through song, we internalize these core beliefs, allowing them to shape our worldview and guide our actions.

2. Hymns as Narrative Threads:

Many traditional hymns retell the stories of scripture, bringing to life the triumphs and tragedies of the Bible. We sing of creation in "How Great Thou Art", witness the exodus through "Let My People Go", and experience the passion and resurrection of Christ in countless hymns like ""The Time-Worn Cross" and "Today, Christ the Lord Has Risen". By engaging with these narratives through song, we deepen our understanding of the biblical message and connect with the characters and events on a more personal level.

3. Hymns as Expressions of Emotion:

Traditional hymns offer a powerful outlet for expressing the full spectrum of human emotions in the context of faith. We sing of joy and celebration in hymns like "Joy to the World" and "Sing Hosanna", while lamentations and pleas for forgiveness find voice in hymns like "Amazing Grace" and "Nearer, My God, to Thee". By giving voice to these emotions through song, we connect with the divine on a more intimate level, finding solace, strength, and hope in the shared experience of faith.

4. Hymns as Fostering Community:

Singing together is a communal act, a powerful way to transcend individual differences and unite as a faith community. When we raise our voices in unison, we transcend physical boundaries and become part of something larger than ourselves. Traditional hymns, passed down through generations, connect us to those who came before us and those who will follow, fostering a sense of belonging and shared purpose within the Church.

5. Hymns as Expressions of Cultural Heritage:

Traditional hymns are not merely songs; they are cultural artifacts that reflect the values, traditions, and experiences of the Catholic community throughout history. The language, music, and symbolism embedded within these hymns offer a window into the faith practices and devotional expressions of different eras and regions. By engaging with these hymns, we gain a deeper appreciation for the richness and diversity of the Catholic Church's cultural tapestry.

In Conclusion:

Traditional Catholic hymns are more than just beautiful melodies; they are living expressions of faith, powerful tools for spiritual growth, and enduring symbols of our shared Catholic heritage. As we continue to sing these hymns, let us remember the stories they tell, the emotions they evoke, and the sense of community they foster. May these timeless melodies continue to enrich our faith journey, connect us to the divine, and unite us as a Church for generations to come.

VII

Additional Resources

26

Prayers for the Departed

In the tapestry of our Catholic faith, the threads of life and death are inextricably woven together. While we mourn the loss of loved ones who have passed, our faith assures us that their journey doesn't end here. We believe in the communion of saints, a spiritual connection that transcends the veil between the living and the departed. This belief inspires us to **pray for the departed**, offering them comfort, seeking their intercession, and expressing our enduring love.

1. A Tradition Rooted in Scripture:

The practice of praying for the dead finds its roots in the rich soil of scripture. In the Second Book of Maccabees, we encounter the story of Judas Maccabeus offering prayers and sacrifices for the fallen soldiers, demonstrating an early understanding of the importance of intercessory prayer (2 Maccabees 12:43-46).

This tradition continues throughout the New Testament, with Jesus himself acknowledging the existence of an afterlife and the possibility of communication between the living and the dead (Luke 16:19-31).

2. Expressions of Love and Longing:

Prayers for the departed are not merely empty rituals; they are heartfelt expressions of love and longing. We yearn for our loved ones who have passed, and prayer becomes a bridge that connects us across the divide. Through prayer, we share our grief, express our gratitude for their presence in our lives, and entrust them to God's loving care.

3. Seeking Comfort and Intercession:

Beyond expressing our own emotions, prayers for the departed also offer them comfort and support. We believe that our prayers can reach them in the spiritual realm, offering solace and reminding them of the love that continues to surround them. Additionally, we may seek their intercession, asking them to pray for us before God's throne, drawing strength from their continued presence in the communion of saints.

4. Prayers Rooted in Faith:

Our prayers for the departed are not based on mere speculation or wishful thinking. They are rooted in the firm foundation of our faith. We believe in the transformative power of God's grace, even after death. We pray that our loved ones may be cleansed of any remaining imperfections and welcomed into the fullness of God's love.

5. A Tapestry of Prayers:

The Catholic tradition offers a rich tapestry of prayers for the departed. From the simple and heartfelt "Eternal rest grant unto them, O Lord" to the more elaborate prayers of the Rosary and the Divine Mercy Chaplet, each prayer expresses our love, longing, and faith in the transformative power of God's grace.

6. Praying for All the Faithful Departed:

Our prayers extend beyond our immediate family and friends. We also remember the countless souls who have passed on, known and unknown. We pray for all the faithful departed, entrusting them to God's mercy and imploring His compassion for those who may have died without the comfort of faith or the support of loved ones.

7. A Journey of Hope and Transformation:

Praying for the departed is not simply an act of mourning; it is a journey of hope and transformation. By entrusting our loved ones to God's care, we express our faith in the promise of eternal life and the ultimate victory of love over death. We pray that they may find peace and fulfillment in the presence of God, and that we may one day be reunited with them in the eternal joy of heaven.

Remember, dear reader, praying for the departed is not a mere obligation, but a beautiful expression of love, faith, and hope.

As we weave these prayers into the tapestry of our lives, we strengthen our connection with those who have passed, find solace in our grief, and affirm our belief in the enduring power of God's love that transcends the boundaries of life and death.

27

Prayers for the Sick and Dying

In the tapestry of life, threads of joy and sorrow are intricately woven together. While we celebrate milestones and bask in blessings, we also inevitably encounter moments of illness and the impending reality of death. In these tender times, **prayer becomes a powerful refuge**, offering solace to the afflicted, comfort to loved ones, and a bridge connecting us to the divine.

A Tapestry of Prayers:

The Catholic tradition offers a rich tapestry of prayers specifically designed to **offer support and comfort** to those facing illness and the approach of death. These prayers are not mere words; they are **expressions of love, faith, and hope**, reaching out to God in times of vulnerability and need.

For the Sick:

• **Prayers for Healing:** When illness strikes, we naturally yearn for restoration and wholeness. Prayers for healing can be as simple as offering a heartfelt plea to God for the restoration of health, or they can draw upon specific passages from scripture or traditional prayers like the **Prayer to Saint Michael the Archangel** or the **Chaplet of Divine Mercy.**

• **Prayers for Strength and Comfort:** Beyond physical healing, those battling illness often require immense emotional and spiritual strength. Prayers for strength and comfort can offer solace and peace, reminding the individual that they are not alone in their struggle. Prayers like the **Prayer to the Holy Spirit** or the **Litany of Trust** can provide a sense of calm and inner peace.

• **Prayers for Acceptance:** As the course of illness unfolds, there may come a time for acceptance. Prayers for acceptance can help individuals and their loved ones find peace with the reality of the situation, while still holding onto hope and faith. Prayers like the **Prayer of Saint Francis** or the **Serenity Prayer** can offer guidance and strength during this challenging time.

For the Dying:

• **PrayersforaPeacefulPassing:** Aslifenearsitsend,prayers for a peaceful passing offer comfort and support to both the dying and their loved ones. These prayers can ask for God's presence to ease any fear or anxiety and for a gentle transition into the next life. Prayers like the **Commendatory Prayer** or the **Apostles' Creed** can be recited at the bedside, offering solace and a sense of sacredness.

· **Prayers for Eternal Rest:** After the passing of a loved one, prayers for eternal rest express our hope and belief in the afterlife. These prayers ask for God's mercy and compassion for the deceased, and for their eternal peace in His presence. Prayers like the **Eternal rest grant unto them, O Lord** or the **In Paradisum** can be offered to find comfort
and express our faith in the promise of eternal life.

Beyond Words:
While prayers offer powerful support, it's important to remember that they are not meant to be a replacement for seeking professional medical care or emotional support. However, **prayers can be a powerful complement to these efforts**, provid- ing a sense of spiritual grounding and connection to something larger than ourselves.

Remember, dear reader, in times of illness and loss, you are not alone. The tapestry of faith offers a wealth of prayers to guide you through these challenging moments. Embrace these prayers as a source of comfort, strength, and hope, and allow them to connect you to the divine presence that offers solace and peace in the midst of life's inevitable challenges.

28

Catholic Sacraments: Sources of Grace and Blessings

In the vibrant tapestry of the Catholic faith, the seven sacraments stand as **luminous threads**, woven into the very fabric of our lives. These sacred encounters are not mere rituals, but **channels of divine grace**, offering us a tangible experience of God's love and transformative power. Let us delve into each sacrament, exploring its unique significance and the blessings it bestows upon us.

1. Baptism: The Gateway to Faith

Baptism marks the **dawn of our Christian life**, washing away original sin and welcoming us into the **family of God**. As water touches our foreheads, we are **reborn** in Christ, becoming **children of God** and **inheritors of His Kingdom**. This sacrament grants us **sanctifying grace**, the very life of God within us, and empowers us to live according to His will.

Imagine a magnificent cathedral, its doors tightly shut. Baptism is the key that unlocks these doors, granting us access to the vast riches of God's grace and the vibrant community of faith within the Church.

2. Confirmation: Strengthened by the Spirit

Having entered the Church through baptism, **Confirmation** deepens our connection with God by granting us the **seven gifts of the Holy Spirit**. These virtues, namely wisdom, understand- ing, counsel, fortitude, knowledge, piety, and fear of the Lord, empower us to embody our faith with courage, compassion, and discernment.

Think of Confirmation as a powerful wind beneath our wings, propelling us forward on our Christian journey. The Holy Spirit empowers us to **witness to our faith, resist temptation,** and **grow in holiness.**

3. Eucharist: A Sacred Meal of Love

The **Eucharist**, also known as **Holy Communion**, is the **central pillar of Catholic life**. In this sacred meal, we **receive Jesus Christ** himself, truly present in the **bread and wine** consecrated during the Mass. Through this profound act of **communion**, we are **united with Christ** and nourished by His divine love.

Imagine a magnificent banquet table laden with the finest delicacies. The Eucharist is an invitation to this sacred feast, where we **share in the very life of Christ** and experience the depths of His love in a transformative way.

4. Reconciliation: Forgiveness and Renewal

We are all human, and inevitably, we stumble and fall short. **Reconciliation**, also known as **Confession**, offers us the **gift of God's forgiveness** and the **opportunity for renewal**. By confessing our sins to a priest and receiving his absolution, we are **washed clean** and **restored to God's grace**.

Picture a dusty mirror, reflecting a distorted image. Reconcilia- tion is the cleansing cloth that wipes away the dust, allowing us to see ourselves clearly and **reflect the radiant light of God's love** once again.

5. Anointing of the Sick: Comfort and Healing

When illness or frailty strike, the **Anointing of the Sick** offers **spiritual and physical comfort**. Through the laying on of hands and the anointing with holy oil, God's **healing grace** is poured out upon the recipient, bringing **strength, peace, and hope**.

Imagine a soothing balm applied to a wound. The Anointing of the Sick is a similar act of **divine tenderness**, offering solace and **strengthening the spirit** during times of suffering.

6. Holy Orders: A Call to Serve

For some, God extends a special calling to **serve the Church** in a unique way. Through the sacrament of **Holy Orders**, men are **ordained as priests, deacons, or bishops**. This sacrament equips them with the **grace and authority** to **celebrate the sacraments, preach the Gospel, and lead the faithful**.

Think of a majestic lighthouse, guiding ships safely through treacherous waters. Those ordained through Holy Orders become **instruments of God's grace**, leading others towards the light of faith and the safe harbor of salvation.

7. Matrimony: A Covenant of Love

Marriage, established between a man and a woman through the **sacrament of Matrimony**, is a **sacred covenant** reflecting God's love for His people. This sacrament **sanctifies the marital bond**, granting couples the **grace** to **love each other selflessly, build a Christ-centered family**, and **bear witness to God's love in the world**.

Imagine two flames coming together to create a single, brighter light. Matrimony is the union of two souls, **strengthened by God's grace** to illuminate the world with the radiance of their love.

These seven sacraments are not merely symbolic gestures; they are **powerful encounters with God's grace**, transforming our lives and drawing us closer to Him. As we **participate in these sacred mysteries** with open hearts,

29

Prayers for the World and the Church

The world around us is a vibrant tapestry woven with threads of joy and sorrow, hope and despair. As members of the global community and the Church, we are called to extend our prayers beyond the walls of our homes and communities, embracing the needs of those who suffer and yearning for a world filled with peace, justice, and love.

1. A Prayer for Peace:
O God, Prince of Peace,
We approach You with heavy hearts, weighed down by the conflicts and violence that afflict our world. We see innocent lives lost, families shattered, and communities torn apart. We pray for an end to all wars and hostilities, for a world where swords are beaten into plowshares and spears into pruning hooks.
Grant wisdom to leaders, guiding them towards peaceful

resolutions and fostering dialogue and understanding. Fill the hearts of all with compassion and a yearning for reconcilia- tion. May the weapons of war be silenced and replaced by the instruments of peace: love, forgiveness, and justice.
Amen.

2. A Prayer for Justice:
Almighty God, source of all righteousness,
We lift up our voices in prayer for those who suffer from injustice and oppression. We see the marginalized and forgotten, the voiceless and powerless, yearning for a world where justice prevails. We pray for an end to discrimination, prejudice, and all forms of inequality.

Grant courage to those who fight for justice, empowering them to speak truth to power and advocate for the rights of all. Inspire hearts with compassion and a commitment to building a society rooted in fairness and equality. May the scales of justice be balanced, ensuring dignity and respect for every human being.
Amen.

3. A Prayer for the Needs of the Global Community:
Everlasting God, our compassionate Father,
We come before You with a heavy heart, burdened by the suffering and challenges faced by our global community. We see poverty, hunger, disease, and natural disasters wreaking havoc on countless lives. We pray for those affected by these hardships, offering them comfort and hope in their time of
need.
Grant wisdom and resources to those working tirelessly to alleviate suffering and bring relief to those in need. Inspire

121

generosity in the hearts of many, prompting them to share their blessings and extend a helping hand to their brothers and sisters across the globe. May Your love and compassion guide our actions, fostering a world where all can live with dignity and hope.
Amen.

4. A Prayer for the Church:
O God, head of the Church,
We lift up our beloved Church in prayer, entrusting it to Your loving care. Grant wisdom and guidance to our leaders, empowering them to shepherd Your flock with compassion and integrity. Strengthen the unity of the Church, fostering love and understanding among all its members.

Inspire a renewed sense of purpose and mission within the Church, calling us to be instruments of Your love and compas- sion in the world. May the Church be a beacon of hope, offering solace to the afflicted, advocating for the marginalized, and sharing the message of Your love with all.
Amen.

Beyond the Words:
These prayers are mere starting points, offered as a founda-tion for your own heartfelt expressions. As you pray for the world and the Church, allow your heart to connect with the suffering and needs of others. Feel the call to compassion and action, recognizing that each of us has a role to play in building a more just and peaceful world.

Remember, prayer is not a passive act, but a powerful force

for change. As we lift up our voices in prayer, we connect with a community of believers united in hope and compassion. Together, we can weave a tapestry of hope and love, one prayer at a time, striving to make the world a better place for all.

30

Prayers from the Saints and Spiritual Traditions

The tapestry of Christian faith is woven with countless threads, each representing the unique voices and experiences of believ- ers throughout history. Among these threads, the prayers of the saints and spiritual giants shine brightly, offering timeless expressions of devotion, wisdom, and hope. As we delve into these cherished prayers, we connect not only with the individuals who penned them, but also with the universal yearnings of the human spirit.

1. The Serenity Prayer (Saint Francis of Assisi):
   > "Grant me the strength to accept what I cannot control,
>The courage to change what I can,
>And the wisdom to know the difference."

This simple yet profound prayer, attributed to Saint Francis of Assisi, encapsulates a core principle of Christian faith: acceptance, courage, and wisdom. It acknowledges the limitations of human control while emphasizing the importance of inner strength and discernment in navigating life's challenges.

2. A Prayer for Peace (Saint Augustine):
> "O Lord, our God, **Let us strive for peace within, among each other, and across the world."**

Saint Augustine's prayer for peace resonates deeply in a world often marked by conflict and division. It extends beyond individual well-being, encompassing a yearning for peace within families, communities, and across the globe. This prayer serves as a powerful reminder of our collective responsibility to
foster harmony and understanding.

3. A Prayer for Guidance (Saint Teresa of Avila):
> "Let nothing disturb you,
> Let nothing frighten you,
> All things are passing,
> God never changes.
> Patience obtains all things.
> Whoever has God, lacks nothing;
> God alone suffices."

Saint Teresa of Avila's prayer offers solace and reassurance in the face of life's uncertainties. It reminds us of God's enduring presence and the impermanence of earthly troubles. By placing our faith in God and cultivating patience, we are assured that all things will ultimately work out according to His divine plan.

4. A Prayer for Love (Saint John of the Cross):
> "Let nothing possess you, let nothing come near you
> That is not God, or that does not bring you to God."

Saint John of the Cross, a renowned mystic, emphasizes the centrality of divine love in his prayer. He encourages us to detach from worldly possessions and desires, focusing instead on cultivating a deeper relationship with God. This prayer serves as a call to prioritize our spiritual well-being and seek true fulfillment in the love of God.

5. A Prayer for Gratitude (Brother David):

> "Thank you for the world so beautiful,
> For the sun and the moon and the rain.
> Thank you for the music and the laughter,
> Thank you for pain."

Brother David's prayer expresses profound gratitude for the richness and complexity of life's experiences. He acknowledges not only the joys and blessings, but also the challenges and hardships, recognizing that each contributes to our growth and understanding. This prayer encourages us to cultivate an attitude of gratitude in all circumstances, trusting in God's providence.

Beyond the Words:

These prayers from the saints and spiritual traditions are more than mere historical artifacts; they are living testaments to the enduring power of faith. As we recite them, we connect with the hearts and minds of individuals who have walked a similar path, finding solace, strength, and inspiration in their communion with God.

Remember, dear reader, these prayers are not meant to be merely memorized and recited; they are invitations to personal reflection and dialogue with the divine. Allow their words to resonate within your heart, inspiring your own expressions of faith, hope, and love. As you do so, you become part of the ongoing tapestry of prayer woven by countless believers throughout history, contributing your unique voice to the chorus of faith that echoes across the ages.

VIII

Conclusion

31

Embracing a Life of Prayer and Devotion

As we reach the end of our exploration of the Daily Missal and its treasures, a profound question lingers: **how can we translate these sacred words and rituals into a life lived in prayer and devotion?** The answer, dear reader, lies not in grand gestures or complicated formulas, but in the **quiet, consistent choices** we make each day.

1. Cultivating a Habit of Prayer:
The first step on this journey is **developing a regular practice of prayer**. This doesn't have to be an overwhelming endeavor. Start small, perhaps with a few minutes of **Morning Prayer** each day. As you become comfortable with this routine, gradually add other forms of prayer, such as **evening prayer, meditation, or Lectio Divina**. Remember, consistency is key. Even a few minutes of focused prayer each day can have a transformative impact on your life.

2. Integrating Prayer into Daily Life:

Prayer doesn't have to be confined to designated times or specific locations. **Weave moments of prayer throughout your day.** Offer a **silent prayer of gratitude** before a meal, **petition God for guidance** before making a difficult decision, or simply **express your worries and joys** to Him in a quiet conversation. By integrating prayer into the fabric of your daily life, you create a constant dialogue with God, keeping Him present in every aspect of your existence.

3. The Power of the Sacraments:

The **sacraments** are not mere rituals; they are **channels of God's grace**, offering us nourishment and strength on our spiritual journey. **Regular participation in the Mass** is essential for fostering a deeper connection with God and the Church community. Additionally, **seeking the sacrament of Reconciliation** allows us to experience God's forgiveness and healing love, while **receiving the Eucharist** provides us with spiritual sustenance and strengthens our union with Christ.

4. Living a Life of Service:

True devotion extends beyond personal prayer and piety. It manifests in **acts of love and service** towards others. As Jesus himself instructed, **"love one another as I have loved you"** (John 13:34). Look for opportunities to **extend a helping hand** to those in need, whether it's volunteering your time, offering a kind word, or simply showing compassion to someone struggling. By serving others, we not only alleviate their suffering but also **reflect the love of Christ** in the world.

5. A Journey of Continuous Growth:

Remember, dear reader, the path of prayer and devotion is not a destination, but a **lifelong journey**. There will be moments of **doubt and discouragement**, times when prayer feels like an empty exercise. However, **perseverance is key**. Trust in God's presence, even when you don't feel it, and **seek guidance from spiritual mentors** and the Church community. As you continue to nurture your faith through prayer, reflection, and service, you will experience a **deepening relationship with God** and a **transformation in your own life**.

In conclusion, embracing a life of prayer and devotion is not about achieving some unattainable state of holiness. It's about cultivating a relationship with God, one conversation, one act of service, one step at a time. By incorporating these practices into your daily life, you embark on a beautiful journey of spiritual growth, transformation, and service, ultimately drawing closer to the God who loves you uncondi- tionally.

IX

Appendices

32

Glossary of Liturgical Terms

Welcome, fellow pilgrim on the path of faith! As you delve deeper into the rich tapestry of Catholic liturgy, you may encounter unfamiliar terms and concepts. Fear not, for this glossary serves as your friendly guide, offering clear and concise explanations to illuminate your understanding.

1. **Altar:** The central focus of the church, representing the **sacrificial table** where Christ's offering is made present during the Eucharist. It symbolizes the **communion between God and humanity.**

2. **Ambo:** Theelevatedplatformfromwhichthe**WordofGod** is proclaimed. It signifies the **importance of Scripture** in the life of the Church.

3. **Celebrant:** The ordained minister who presides over the liturgy, typically a priest or deacon. He acts as the **visible sign of Christ** leading the community in prayer and worship.

4. **Chalice:** The cup used to hold the consecrated wine during the Eucharist, symbolizing the **blood of Christ**. It is a sacred vessel representing the **gift of redemption**.

5. **Ciborium:** A sacred vessel used to hold consecrated bread (hosts) for distribution during Communion. It signifies the **abundance of God's grace** available to all believers.

6. **Deacon:** An ordained minister who assists the priest in various liturgical functions. He serves as a **bridge between the clergy and the laity**, proclaiming the Gospel, assisting with Communion, and offering prayers.

7. **Eucharist:** The central sacrament of the Catholic Church, also known as Holy Communion. It is the **re-presentation of Christ's sacrifice** through the bread and wine, which become His body and blood.

8. **Gospel:** One of the four canonical accounts of the life and teachings of Jesus Christ. It is proclaimed during the Mass and serves as a **source of inspiration and guidance** for the faithful.

9. **Homily:** The reflection or sermon given by the celebrant after the readings, offering **insights and interpretations** of the Scripture passages and their relevance to daily life.

10. **Incense:** A fragrant smoke used during certain liturgical celebrations, symbolizing **prayer ascending to heaven**. It signifies **reverence and devotion** towards God.

11. **Lectern:** A stand holding the book of readings used during the liturgy. It signifies the **importance of Scripture** in the life of the Church.

12. **Lectionary:** A book containing the readings chosen for each day of the liturgical year. It ensures that the **rich tapestry of Scripture** is proclaimed throughout the year.

13. **Litany:** A form of prayer consisting of a series of petitions

and responses, often used to invoke the intercession of saints or for specific needs. It encourages **communal prayer and intercession**.

14. **Offertory:** The part of the Mass where the bread and wine are presented, signifying the **offering of ourselves and our gifts to God**. It reflects our **participation in Christ's sacrifice**.

15. **Pall:** A square cloth used to cover the chalice during the Eucharist. It signifies **reverence for the consecrated elements**.

16. **Paten:** A plate used to hold the bread (host) during the Eucharist before consecration. It represents the **altar of sacrifice** upon which Christ offered Himself.

17. **Penitential Rite:** The opening part of the Mass where we acknowledge our sins and seek God's forgiveness. It prepares our hearts for **worthy reception of the Eucharist**.

18. **Sign of Peace:** A gesture of peace and reconciliation exchanged among the faithful during the Mass. It signifies the **unity and love** that should characterize the Christian community.

19. **Vestments:** The special garments worn by clergy during liturgical celebrations. They represent the **sacredness of the occasion** and the **roles of the different ministers**.

20. **Sanctuary:** The area around the altar, considered the most sacred space within the church. It signifies the **presence of God** and the **heavenly realm**.

Remember, dear reader, this glossary is just a starting point on your liturgical journey. As you continue to explore and participate in the rich tapestry of Catholic worship, these terms will become more than just words; they will become signposts guiding you deeper into the mystery of faith and the beauty of the Catholic tradition.

33

Index of Prayers and Hymns: A Gateway to Sacred Encounter

As the sun paints the morning sky, casting its golden hues across our world, countless Catholics across the globe embark on a beautiful tradition: **connecting with the Divine** through the rich tapestry of **prayers and hymns**. This index serves as your guide, a compass pointing towards the countless ways we, as a faith community, can **nurture our relationship with God** through the power of words and song.

A Treasury of Prayers:

Within the vast realm of Catholic prayer lies a treasure trove waiting to be explored. Here, we delve into some of the most cherished and transformative prayers:

> • **Morning Prayer (Lauds):** As the first rays of dawn kiss the horizon, many faithful gather to greet the day with **Lauds**, a prayer service acknowledging God's presence

and surrendering the day to His will. Through Psalms, scripture readings, and hymns, hearts are lifted in praise and thanksgiving.

• **The Rosary:** This meditative prayer, often recited with the aid of rosary beads, invites us to contemplate the mysteries of faith. As we journey through the joyful, sorrowful, glorious, and luminous mysteries, we deepen our understanding of Christ's life, ministry, and sacrifice.

• **The Liturgy of the Hours:** This prayer cycle, encompassing Lauds, Vespers, Compline, and other hours, provides a rhythm of prayer throughout the day. By integrating scripture, psalms, and intercessions into our daily routines, we remain connected to God throughout the ebb and flow of life.

• **Liturgical Prayers:** The Mass, the central act of Catholic worship, is woven with a tapestry of prayers. From the opening Penitential Act to the concluding Prayer after Communion, these prayers guide us through confession, thanksgiving, and petition, fostering a profound encounter with the Divine.

• **Personal Prayers:** Beyond the structured forms, lies the sacred space of personal prayer. This is where hearts converse directly with God, sharing joys, sorrows, anxieties, and aspirations. Whether whispered in the quiet of our homes or uttered in the stillness of nature, these intimate dialogues nourish our relationship with the Divine.

Hymns: Songs of the Soul

Just as prayers are expressions of our hearts, hymns are the **melodic outpourings of our souls.** They elevate our voices in praise, weave stories of faith, and offer solace in times of need.

Let us explore the different categories of hymns that enrich our worship:

· **Seasonal Hymns:** Throughout the liturgical year, specific hymns resonate with the unique character of each season. From the expectant joy of Advent carols to the triumphant anthems of Easter, these hymns guide us through the Church's calendar, deepening our understanding of the mysteries we celebrate.

· **Sacramental Hymns:** As we partake in the sacred rituals of the Church, specific hymns accompany these moments of grace. From the hushed reverence of Eucharistic hymns to the joyful melodies of baptismal songs, these hymns enhance the experience of the sacraments, drawing us deeper into their spiritual significance.

· **Marian Hymns:** Holding a special place in the hearts of Catholics, hymns dedicated to the Blessed Virgin Mary express devotion, love, and gratitude. These hymns, whether contemplative or celebratory, remind us of Mary's role as intercessor and mother of the Church.

· **Hymns of Praise and Thanksgiving:** From the majestic grandeur of "How Great Thou Art" to the simple beauty of "Thank You, Lord," hymns of praise and thanksgiving overflow with gratitude for God's countless blessings. These songs lift our spirits, reminding us of His constant presence and love.

· **Hymns of Petition and Intercession:** When faced with challenges or seeking guidance, we turn to hymns of petition and intercession. These songs carry our prayers to God, expressing our needs, hopes, and desires for ourselves and the world around us.

Beyond the Index: A Journey of Faith

This index is merely a starting point, a gateway to the vast and enriching world of Catholic prayers and hymns. As you delve deeper into this sacred realm, remember that the true essence lies not just in the words and melodies, but in the **intentional encounter with the Divine** they facilitate. Allow these prayers and hymns to be the bridge connecting your heart to God, fostering a deeper relationship built on love, gratitude, and unwavering faith.

Remember, dear reader, this journey of faith is not a solitary one. As you explore the prayers and hymns within this index, know that you are joining a chorus of voices across generations and continents, all united in their love for The desire to grow closer to God and deepen one's connection with Him. So, let your voice join the symphony, allowing these sacred expressions to guide you on your lifelong pilgrimage of faith.

34

Acknowledgments: A Heartfelt Expression of Gratitude

As I reach the culmination of this work, a profound sense of gratitude washes over me. This book, much like the tapestry of faith it explores, is not solely the product of my own endeavors. It is a testament to the countless individuals who, in their unique ways, have contributed to its creation and success.

To my family and friends, your unwavering support has been the bedrock upon which this journey was built. You have offered encouragement during moments of doubt, celebrated milestones with genuine joy, and provided a listening ear whenever needed. Your love and belief in me have been the fuel that propelled me forward.

To my spiritual mentors, your guidance and wisdom have been invaluable. You have challenged me to delve deeper into my faith, shared your own insights, and offered prayers that sustained me throughout this process. Your dedication to nurturing my spiritual growth has left an indelible mark on this work.

To my editor and publishing team, your expertise and dedica- tion have been instrumental in bringing this book to life. You have meticulously combed through every sentence, offering invaluable suggestions and ensuring clarity and coherence in the final product. Your collaborative spirit and unwavering commitment to excellence have been truly inspiring.

To the countless scholars and theologians whose works I have drawn upon, your research and insights have served as the foundation upon which I have built. Your dedication to exploring the intricacies of faith has enriched my understanding and allowed me to share these insights with others.

To my readers, your willingness to embark on this journey with me is humbling and deeply appreciated. I pray that the words within these pages resonate with your hearts, spark meaningful reflection, and offer a deeper connection to the richness of our faith.

Finally, to God, the ultimate source of all wisdom and inspira- tion, I express my deepest gratitude. You have guided my steps, granted me the strength to persevere, and filled me with the grace to share this gift with the world. May this work serve as an instrument to glorify Your name and inspire others to draw closer to You.

This expression of gratitude extends beyond mere words. It is a heartfelt acknowledgment of the interconnectedness that binds us together, a testament to the power of collaboration, and a celebration of the shared journey of faith. As you turn the final page, dear reader, may you carry with you the spirit of gratitude and allow it to ripple outward, enriching your own life and the lives of those around you.

Made in the USA
Las Vegas, NV
08 April 2024

88417415R00085